D1535205

Lincoln and the Emperors

A. R. Tyrner-Tyrnauer

Lincoln and the Emperors

Harcourt, Brace & World, Inc.

NEW YORK

TO MY DAUGHTER ALICE GABRIELLE

without whose assistance, encouragement,
and devotion this book
would never have been written

Acknowledgments

I WISH TO EXPRESS MY indebtedness to Director General Hofrat Gebhard Rath of the Austrian State Archives (the former House, Court, and State Archives of the Habsburg Emperors) where most of my researches for *Lincoln and the Emperors* were carried on. Hofrat Rath's great knowledge and amiable helpfulness considerably facilitated my work in these unique archives. Thanks are also due to his entire staff, in particular to his efficient assistant Dr. Rudolf Neck.

On this side of the Atlantic I am indebted to our outstanding Lincoln scholar, Mr. Bruce Catton, for his generous encouragement, and to Dr. Fritz T. Epstein for his expert guidance through the Library of Congress.

I owe a great deal to the invaluable assistance and constructive suggestions of my daughter Alice Gabrielle, to the judicious advice of my wise bibliophile-philosopher friend Dr. Walter Eckstein, and to the cheerful co-operation of my wife Erna during my prolonged relapse into the nineteenth century.

Finally, my gratitude is due to all those who have helped me to appreciate Lincoln the humane warrior and to understand his unique position in the history of the last hundred years.

Contents

x

XIV

XV

Introduction

AMONG THE INNUMERABLE BOOKS on Lincoln and the Civil War are monumental biographies and impressive historical accounts. But both biographers and historians seem to have ignored—or at least underrated—the fact that, socially and politically, America is an offspring of Europe.

While doing some research in connection with the centenary of the Civil War, I was amazed to find that there is not a single book in the vast Lincoln literature dealing adequately with the European background of the great conflict. Some authors treat it as a side line to the history of an indigenous war engendered by indigenous causes, but they all overlook the common source: the struggle between the nineteenth-century Industrial Revolution and the bitterly resisting forces of the incumbent Old Order.

I transferred my research to Europe, in particular to the famous Vienna House, Court, and State Archives, repository of the formerly confidential records of the Imperial House of Habsburg. Except for the far less accessible

Archives of the Vatican, the Vienna Archives house the most universal records relevant to the history of the Western world. Chronologically these documents cover more than eleven centuries, and they fill a space of more than seventeen thousand cubic meters (approximately six hundred thousand cubic feet). Several months of intensive research in this historic gold mine yielded 471 items (diplomatic documents, high-level secret correspondence, and intelligence reports relating to the period of the Civil War).

Of the available documents of the period in the Vienna Archives, nearly 90 per cent were written in French, the diplomatic language of the nineteenth century. Of the important documents, only some interdynastic correspondence, as between Emperor Francis Joseph I and his brother Maximilian, or Leopold I, the King of the Belgians, and his son-in-law Maximilian, was in German, and of course Lincoln's and Seward's letters were in English. In the letters in English, by the way, the spelling in the originals has been retained.

As the Civil War occurred before the invention of the first practical typewriter, all documents were in longhand—a few in beautiful calligraphy, but many in eye-taxing, small, and almost illegible handwriting.

Also a number of the listed documents have disappeared, owing to wartime dispersion of the Archives material. Fearing a bombardment of Vienna during the last phase of World War II, government officials hid the invaluable documents in the cellars of ancient castles and monasteries outside the capital. Only a small fraction was damaged by bombs or fire, but a considerable part of the so-called Maximilian Archives was misplaced and was found only after many years of exploration in the nearly ten-mile-long shelf-catacombs of the Archives.

Because of limitations of space in this one-volume book, it has not been possible to include all documents in full translation. It is to be hoped, however, that further research in the international background of the Civil War will result in other volumes dedicated to a better understanding of the interrelation of America with the rest of the world.

DURING THE LINCOLN PERIOD the European empires made a last attempt to regain their hold over North America and to reintroduce the "monarchic principle" into that "dangerous hotbed of republicanism." Emperor Francis Joseph I of Austria had an additional, personal interest in the outcome of the American Civil War. On it hinged the existence of a new Habsburg realm and the very life of his younger brother, Emperor Maximilian of Mexico, whose greatest American antagonist was President Lincoln and whose natural allies were the states of the South. Both Francis Joseph and Maximilian, like most other crowned heads of their time, saw in Lincoln the personification of the republican ideas that had kindled the antimonarchist revolutions in Europe. They naturally hated and feared Lincoln and hoped that the Civil War would destroy, or at least weaken, the United States of America.

The Civil War was not a "homespun" affair. It was the result of the same upheavals that have changed the face of Europe, and the interrelations are clearly mirrored in the Archives documents. The promises and active help of the European empires had stiffened the attitude of the Southern leaders, some of whom were quite willing to see the monarchic principle triumph in North America.

During the first year of the Civil War, Napoleon III —and his Empress Eugénie—took the initiative in forming a European coalition for intervention in favor of the South. He also was chiefly responsible for turning Mexico into a French-Austrian protectorate under Maximilian of Habsburg, supported by a French army of occupation, which of course represented a potential threat to the Union.

Francis Joseph, who at the beginning of his long reign was preoccupied with suppressing national and republican revolutions, gave his approval to Napoleon's schemes and his blessing to Maximilian's adventure. He was, however, far more cautious and conservative than the "upstart" Emperor of the French, whom he heartily distrusted.

Queen Victoria's Prime Minister, Lord Palmerston, was for intervention and recognition of the Confederacy. He was particularly interested in reducing the stature of the Union and in increasing cotton imports from the blockaded South, since England's textile industries were suffering from cotton famine.

Ironically, the most autocratic of all European empires, Russia, opposed recognition of the Confederacy and gave assurances of support to the Union government. Czar Alexander II had abolished serfdom in his country almost simultaneously with the outbreak of the Civil War, but the principal reason for his attitude was British-French intervention in favor of Turkey in the Crimean War (1853-56), which had checked Russia's expansion in southeastern Europe. Another irony of history was that Prussia's Prince Bismarck, who detested Lincoln and expressed sympathy for the South, contributed indirectly more than any other European statesman to the triumph of the Republic and to the final fiasco of the emperors who had opposed Lincoln.

The tragic death of President Lincoln shocked even his enemies, as may be seen in the imperial documents, but the great struggle was already decided and the monarchic principle was doomed. Emperor Maximilian made a last futile attempt at *rapprochement* with Lincoln's successor, President Andrew Johnson—and then the three emperors went down to defeat. A new chapter in history was opened, which was marked by the ascendancy of the United States and the gradual dissolution of the Empires of Europe.

Lincoln and the Emperors

I AMERICA'S LOG CABIN AND
Europe's imperial palace
were both swept away by the Industrial Revolution and
the ensuing chain reactions. Gone are the frontiersman and
the emperor, the hand loom and the slave, the horse and
the arrow, smallpox, puerperal fever, and the minuet.

Human life-span has doubled, and oil, electricity, and
nuclear energy have replaced slave labor. Population has
rapidly increased, breeding more disease and misery but
also more geniuses and healers. Old instruments of produc-
tion and war have become museum exhibits, and this is likely
to happen to horses, too. Royalty has survived—at least in
the Western World—mainly as a social ornament.

The path of human progress (or whatever designation
you prefer for the rapidly increasing rhythm of history)
is hewn by violent social explosions, revolutions, counter-
revolutions, wars, and civil wars. The stretch beginning

3

with the American and French Revolutions at the end of the eighteenth century and leading up to the two world wars—with the Soviet Revolution sandwiched in between —was marked by the most profound changes of any period in history. Empires collapsed, new powers emerged, a rising urban life rapidly displaced rural hegemony, the *ancien régime* crumbled, decayed, and finally gave way, but not without desperate resistance and counterattacks.

Halfway between the great eighteenth- and twentieth-century eruptions the American Civil War, with its far-reaching and vastly underrated global implications, changed the path and rhythm of history. Its outbreak coincided with the bitter struggle between the national-democratic revolutions and the defenders of the Old Order in the Western world. It reached its dramatic climax with the last attempt of the European empires to regain control over their lost American colonies. As one crowned head put it, the Civil War gave Europe's rulers a chance to reintroduce "the monarchic-aristocratic principle" into republican America.[1]

THE *ancien régime* HAD been tottering ever since its defeat by the despised colonists in America and the "unspeakable rabble" in France. The struggle continued for several generations with varying fortunes. Yet time was on the side of the pioneering colonists and the footloose "rabble," the very elements needed by the new industrial-commercial society based on enterprise and change. Their attack upon the rigid class-and-caste system of rural aristocracy was launched under the flags of liberty, equality, nationalism, and democracy. Their opponents raised the standards of legitimism, tradition, birthright, and absolutism.

[1] King Leopold I of Belgium to Archduke Ferdinand Maximilian, October 25, 1861.

The most successful counterattack of the *ancien régime* took place during the first half of the nineteenth century with the establishment of the Holy Alliance of European monarchs. Its chief architect was Prince Clemens Wenzel Metternich-Winneburg, Chancellor of the Austrian Empire. Metternich, who was for more than thirty years the most powerful statesman of the Old World, had one transcendent aim: the restoration and preservation of absolute monarchy, which was destroyed by the French Revolution and its hybrid offspring Napoleon I. Prince Metternich restored the Bourbons in France and even the Inquisition in Spain. He incorporated a part of Italy in the Austrian Empire and was instrumental in wiping Poland off the map. He suppressed all nationalist-democratic movements and encouraged the last vestiges of feudalism, such as serfdom, in central Europe.

The *ancien régime*, however, was not restricted to Europe. There was a landed aristocracy in America as well, even though its claim to supremacy was acquired rather than inherited.

FEW OF THE American colonists were descended from the nobility of Europe. But many of them brought along the social pattern of their old countries together with their sundry beliefs and prejudices and an ambition to move to the top of the social ladder. Climate and soil conditions in the Southern states contributed to the development of a large landowner class which, in the absence of serfs, adopted slavery for its needs. This imitation aristocracy in the South watched the strengthening of the industrial North with no less alarm than its European counterpart, the "genuine" *ancien régime*. To the knights of the Holy Alliance industrial America was a potential inciter and crafty supporter of all republican revolutions. To the ruling caste of the South, on the other hand, the

5

democratic system, championed by the immigration-swollen North, was a tricky device to upset the existing order by the rule of majority.

There was, of course, no "monolithic" North nor a firmly united South in America. The great Virginian, Thomas Jefferson, and many other prominent Southern aristocrats opposed slavery as well as entail and primogeniture, whereas the labor practices of many Northern industrialists were little better than slavery.

Once established, however, slavery became the basis of the plantation economy of the South. The large tobacco and cotton plantations were dependent on slave labor, and the slave owners, much like feudal nobles in Europe, ran the affairs of their respective states. The poorer, nonslaveholding Southern whites often surrendered their majority rights for protection against outlaws, abolitionists and Indians—frequently equated in the sectional mind. As the keenly observant Washington envoy of His Imperial Majesty Francis Joseph I of Austria, Chevalier Johann Georg von Huelsemann, said in one of his reports to Vienna, the attitude of the South had been predetermined by "the great wealth of the plantation owners, consisting of four million slaves, that is four billion dollars." [2]

NOR DID THE monarchs of Europe constitute a united fraternity. Dynastic rivalries continued even during the regal years of the Holy Alliance. The weakened condition of the erstwhile powerful Ottoman Empire encouraged inheritance seekers, which included the entire family of European rulers. The insurrection of the Greeks gave a welcome opportunity for a series of armed interventions. England and France defeated the Sultan's fleet in 1827, and Russia invaded Turkey.

[2] Chevalier Huelsemann to Austrian Foreign Minister Count Rechberg-Rothenloewen, January 23, 1860.

6

Austria cast a covetous eye on the Danubian Provinces straining at the Turkish leash, and, in order to prevent the establishment of a Greek republic, Germany supplied one of her many princes for the newly created Hellenic throne (Otto, second son of King Louis I of Bavaria). A few years later the British and French rulers declared war on their "beloved Brother-Monarch," the Czar of Russia, to check his growing appetite at the Sultan's expense. After the Crimean War, Napoleonic France fought Francis Joseph's Austria for European hegemony, and later both the French and Austrian Empires were defeated by Bismarck's Prussia.[3]

Incidentally, these wars—interrelated with the miscarried effort to "monarchize" America—were the last European conflicts to be settled without United States intervention.

NINETEENTH-CENTURY wars caused but relatively minor shifts in the balance of power. Great revolutionary upheavals, on the other hand, which threatened the existence of monarchy, tended to unite the dynasties of Europe. Such a revolutionary wave rolled over Europe in 1848, brought an end to the reign of the Bourbon-Orléans dynasty in France, and threatened the rule of the Habsburgs. Kings fled, abdicated, promised quick reforms while republican uprisings in Paris, Vienna, Budapest, Prague, Berlin, Munich, Milan, Venice, Rome, the Papal States, Sicily, Poland, Ireland, and other points in the Old World presaged the coming of a new era.

But not yet; the revolutions were suppressed one by one.

Prince Louis Napoleon, nicknamed Napoleon the Little by his adversaries, returned from exile and at the end

[3] Crimean War, 1853-56; Austro-Prussian War, 1866; Franco-Prussian War, 1870-71.

of 1848 managed to get elected on a democratic platform as President of the French Republic. Following the example of his famous uncle, he soon gained complete control of the army, assumed dictatorial power, overturned the Second Republic, and in November, 1852—confirmed by a plebiscite—he proclaimed himself Emperor.

While the guns of 1848 were blazing in Vienna, Prince Metternich, the pride and brains of the *ancien régime*, shed his power and titles and, in the humble disguise of a Herr Meier, fled to England. His Emperor, Ferdinand I, who had been too weak to oppose either Metternich or the rebels, abdicated in favor of his eighteen-year-old nephew, Francis Joseph.

But youth, in this case, meant no change and, least of all, liberal reform. Francis Joseph I was old enough to wear a crown, but still young enough to be under the tutelage of his mother, Archduchess Sophie, "the bigot," as well as of the imperial court, determined to fight for absolutism. The new ruler was to be a figurehead whose throne was extremely precarious, as indicated by Emperor Ferdinand's parting words when Francis Joseph thanked him for handing over the scepter and the crown on December 2, 1848: "Don't mention it, Franzl, it was a real pleasure."

Francis Joseph did what he was told to do: he sanctioned the cruel suppression of the uprisings, and when his generals failed to crush the young Hungarian Republic he called on Czar Nicholas I of Russia to send military aid. The armies of the two Emperors finally triumphed over the poorly equipped forces of Hungary's Lajos Kossuth, the republican leader who had dared to challenge the might of the House of Habsburg. Kossuth fled in August, 1849, but thirteen of his co-leaders of the Revolution were executed. The suppression of the short-lived Hungarian Republic was followed by an era of severe repressions. Herr Meier resumed his princely titles and returned to Austria at the invitation of the Emperor in 1851. Vienna once again became the rallying point of the *ancien régime.*

THE ANTIPODAL RALLYING POINT
on which Europe's revolutionists pinned their hopes was the great Republic across the Atlantic. Fighting rebels looked to Washington for encouragement, and defeated rebels for asylum. They got both in full measure; there were thousands of resolutions, demonstrations, collections, and even some diplomatic conflicts in favor of the soldiers and exiles of 1848.

The year of the revolution in Europe was the year of the gold rush in America. The discovery of gold in California gave a powerful impetus to the westward movement of the growing population and provided an outlet for some of the restless energies of the Atlantic states. New states were being formed in the West, and rivalry for the control of the new territories sharpened the conflict between South and North. In the same year of 1848, defeated Mexico ceded claims to Texas, California, Arizona, New Mexico, Nevada, Utah, and part of Colorado. Apparently all obstacles to the gigantic expansion of the United States were surmounted—but the sudden wealth increased dissension within and jealousy abroad.

Internal discord began to crystallize around slavery and states' rights: abolitionists struck at the core of rural aristocracy by demanding the liberation of slaves. Slaveholders defended their control of the Southern states by challenging the power of the Federal government.

Yet in the field of foreign policy, the young Republic became conscious of its power, stretched its muscles, and pursued an independent—and at times aggressive—foreign policy. European exiles were welcomed and feted in America, and President Fillmore even dispatched a naval vessel to bring "fugitive" Kossuth—for whose capture a reward

9

was posted by the Vienna government—from Turkey to America. When Chevalier Huelsemann protested, Secretary of State Daniel Webster gave expression to the prevalent feeling: "The power of this republic at the present moment is spread over a region, one of the richest and most fertile of the globe, and of an extent in comparison of which the possessions of the House of Habsburg are but as a patch on the earth's surface."[4] The indignant Chevalier threatened severance of diplomatic connections, but Webster's death in 1852 enabled Huelsemann to resume normal relations with the State Department without loss of face.

THE AUSTRIAN ENVOY came from a wealthy but not aristocratic family. He was knighted by Emperor Francis Joseph I in 1852 in recognition of his services at what was then considered a remote and undesirable diplomatic post. He had been sent to Washington in 1838 as a secretary of the Legation and—indicative of the low diplomatic rating of the United States at the time—the young diplomat was in charge of the Legation for several years after the old Austrian Minister's death in 1841. Not until January, 1853, was Huelsemann formally accredited as "Chargé d'Affaires of His Imperial, Royal, and Apostolic Majesty near the Government of the United States," and it was only in 1855 that he was appointed Minister Resident.

But his long sojourn in the United States gave the stocky ex-commoner an advantage over most of his fellow diplomats in Washington. Huelsemann knew America and its people well, and his judgment and foresight far surpassed those of the aristocratic excellencies representing other European powers. Of course, Huelsemann's sympathies were with the South. He served his Emperor and the *ancien régime* loyally. At the same time he kept his eyes open, and his reports were not unduly slanted.

[4] *Congressional Record*, 31st Congress, Senate, Second Session.

Huelsemann faithfully reported every major event that contributed to the growing schism between North and South. He described the financial difficulties of the government and watched carefully for the signs of spreading rebellion. He was well aware of the disunity within President Buchanan's Cabinet and was informed on Southern preparations for the conflict, such as the sending of "State Commissioners" on a secret diplomatic mission to Europe. He deemed civil war unavoidable and predicted international complications arising out of the Republican victory at the 1860 elections. And with misgivings he introduced Abraham Lincoln into the picture, when the little-known, small-town lawyer and former railsplitter was nominated at Chicago in May of the same year.[5]

Huelsemann's portrayal of Lincoln for the benefit of the imperial court of Vienna was not at all flattering. Comparing the new President with Jefferson Davis, head of the newly formed Confederate government, Chevalier Huelsemann found Davis definitely "superior" to Lincoln.[6] But in the course of events the Austrian envoy developed a grudging respect, and even sympathy, for the tall, lanky, inelegant man who emerged from a log cabin to become the symbol of republican democracy and the very antithesis of the Chevalier's revered master, the Emperor by the grace of God.

Abraham Lincoln, the friend of slaves and revolutionaries, was naturally a "menace" to the *ancien régime* in the eyes of the imperial diplomat. But Huelsemann was a correct bureaucrat who knew his place. He sent intelligence and did not assume a policy-making role. Basically he was of a peaceful disposition, unlike his colleagues of the Imperial French Legation who, as Marquis Adolphe de Cham-

[5] Huelsemann to Rechberg, May 8, May 22, November 26, December 17, December 21, December 31, 1860, and January 11, January 15, February 1, 1861.

[6] Huelsemann to Rechberg, February 22, February 25, March 28, 1861.

brun said, had urged their government to recognize the South "and if necessary, declare war on North America." [7]

The envoys, no doubt, reflected their masters' attitudes. By the time Lincoln appeared on the stage of world politics, Emperor Francis Joseph had already learned that the gods of war were unpredictable. His policy therefore was one of caution. On the other hand, Napoleon III stood at the pinnacle of his career, slightly intoxicated by his military successes. In addition, he was a gambler by nature.

[7] Marquis Charles Adolphe de Chambrun, *Impressions of Lincoln and the Civil War.*

II

LINCOLN'S CHIEF AMERICAN adversary, Jefferson Davis, was a typical representative of the imitation aristocracy of the South. Portraits of the two Presidents and their personal backgrounds, superimposed on the social issues of the Civil War, reveal an exquisite irony of history and furnish proof of the environmental formation of human character.

Abraham Lincoln and Jefferson Davis were offspring of the same age, of similar surroundings, and of the same species. They were born only one year (1809 and 1808 respectively) and scarcely more than a hundred miles apart. Each hailed from poor immigrant stock that had come from the British Isles.

The Lincoln family had emigrated from England seven generations before Abe's birth, and the Davises from Wales three or four generations before Jefferson's birth. Both families had settled originally in the North (Massachusetts and Pennsylvania) and both had embarked on a gradual migration to Kentucky in quest of a better life. In Kentucky, an in-between state, the two future Presidents were born of pioneer parents under primitive frontier conditions, but Lincoln in a one-room log cabin and Davis in a double log house of four rooms.

Soon after their birth the environmental differences began. The Lincolns moved northward to Indiana, then to Illinois; the Davises, southward to Mississippi. The Lincolns remained desperately poor and young Abraham experienced all the hardships of destitute frontier life. The Davises, on the other hand, prospered, and little Jeff became the pampered younger brother of the twenty-three-year-older Joseph Davis, who rapidly rose to wealth and prominence among the cotton planters of the Mississippi Valley.

Joseph, as the head of the Davis family, gave Jefferson a gentleman's education and the handsome young man was graduated from West Point in 1828. In the same year Lincoln, with practically no school education, was hired to take a cargo of produce on a flatboat down the Mississippi to New Orleans.

In the Black Hawk War in 1832 they both fought the Indians, Davis as a professional officer and Lincoln as captain of a local militia company. Davis was known as a stern disciplinarian and reckless fighter, whereas Lincoln's outstanding military feat was the rescue from death at the hands of his own men of an old Indian who had wandered into camp with a safe-conduct pass. In 1835 Davis resigned his commission to become a cotton planter on virgin land given to him by his brother. Lincoln meanwhile had managed to make a meager livelihood in a variety of jobs in New Salem. He clerked in a store, went into partnership in still another store, which failed and left him in debt, became postmaster and augmented that job's slim pay by splitting rails, working on farms, assisting at elections, and finally succeeded by hard study in becoming a surveyor. Twice during this period he ran for the State Legislature, winning in his second try in 1834. After his election he studied law in his spare time, and in 1837 began a new career as lawyer in Springfield.

In their active political lives they represented opposing social groups. Davis was a member of Congress briefly in 1845-46 (leaving to head a regiment, the "Mississippi Rifles," in the Mexican War) and Senator from 1847 to 1851 and from 1857 to 1861. From the beginning he was a champion of states' rights, demanding full sovereignty for the states, and a fanatical believer in the Old Order, invoking the Bible to justify slavery. He regarded the Mexican War as a God-given opportunity to extend the Southern slaveholders' empire to the Pacific.

Abraham Lincoln, on the other hand, was elected to Congress in 1847 on the Whig platform, which embraced antislavery. He stood for the supremacy of the Federal Union over the states, and for him secession meant the counterrevolution of a privileged minority. He denounced aggression in general and the Mexican War in particular. He knew that his opposition to the war would cost him many votes and might endanger his political career. Yet when his friend and law partner, William Herndon, warned him against continuing his criticism of the successful war, Lincoln wrote him: "Would you have voted what you felt and knew to be a lie?"

Davis was Secretary of War (1853-57) in President Pierce's Democratic government, strongly influenced by the proslavery Southern plutocrats. Lincoln during these years was one of the principal promoters of the new Republican Party, a popular coalition opposing slavery.

When elected President of the Confederacy, Jefferson Davis, champion of states' rights, restricted these rights to build a strong centralized government. He was above all a war leader and met his defeat at the hands of the pacifist

President of the Union, Abraham Lincoln. The estimated cost of this twin irony of history was half a million human lives and five billions in dollars.

THE ELECTION OF LINCOLN on November 6, 1860, astounded and delighted the *ancien régime* of Europe and its American counterpart in the Southern states. Both realized with a shock the strength of the opposition, which swept to power a scarcely known candidate of the antislavery masses, including numerous refugees and emigrants from imperial Europe. At the same time, European courts and chanceries watched with growing satisfaction the deepening rift within the United States and shared Southern hopes for a chance to reverse the wheel of history.

It was only four days after election that the Legislature of South Carolina summoned a State Convention to give legal sanction to the long-prepared secessionist schemes. And on December 20, 1860, the first Ordinance of Secession was passed. Outgoing President Buchanan's do-nothing attitude encouraged similar movements in other states, and within a few weeks Mississippi, Florida, Alabama, Georgia, and Louisiana followed South Carolina's example. On February 4, 1861, elected delegates of the seceded states—with Texas joining them in a few days—convened at Montgomery, Alabama, adopted a provisional constitution of the Confederate States of America, and on February 9 chose Jefferson Davis provisional President.

Before the end of May, Virginia, Arkansas, Tennessee, and North Carolina had joined the seceded states. As the war unfolded, eleven Southern states faced twenty-three of the North, nine million Southerners—including almost four million slaves—aligned against twenty-three million Northerners with incomparably stronger industrial and financial resources.

The Montgomery convention held its deliberations behind closed doors and the events that took place there have never been clarified. The selection of the site and of the President indicates the preponderant influence of the large cotton-plantation states. And the prominence given foreign affairs at the deliberations is apparent from the appointment of Robert Toombs of Georgia as Secretary of State and the immediate dispatch of agents to Europe to purchase war materials and to try for recognition by the transatlantic powers. Outstanding newsmen Horace Greeley of New York and Edward A. Pollard of Richmond claimed that the Montgomery convention was masterminded by conspiring cotton planters and slaveholders. It is evident that the wealthy planters held the purse strings and were to be the principal beneficiaries of the newly created Confederacy. While the huge income of the planters was derived from the export of cotton, chiefly to England and France, the founders of the Confederacy—planters and politicians alike—were confident of their ability to continue their transatlantic exports despite the threatened blockade by the North. But as the South had neither a navy nor war industry of any importance, the sea lanes could have been kept open only by the ironclads of the big naval powers of Europe, whose help would inevitably have entangled them in a war with the North. So it is reasonable to assume that the Montgomery convention would never have taken its bellicose attitude if it had not been assured in advance that Great Britain and France, and possibly other powers, would recognize and actively support the Confederacy.

This assumption was prevalent in diplomatic circles early in 1861 when Commissioners William Lowndes Yancey, A. Dudley Mann, and Pierre A. Rost began their activities in London and Paris as the quasi Ambassadors of the Confederacy. They were reportedly prepared to go to almost any length to obtain the desired recognition and armed support from the governments of London and Paris. Moreover, their efforts had been prepared by clandestine presecession negotiations between unofficial Southern emissaries and European statesmen.

BIG, BULKY, boisterous Secretary of State Robert Toombs was a lawyer born to cotton riches. A hard drinker, a hard eater, and a hard bargainer, one of the most aggressive orators of the United States Senate, he was also one of the most militant leaders of the South. Toombs had visited Europe in 1855 and had talked to many British and Continental statesmen. He returned as a confirmed admirer of Britain's constitutional monarchy and expressed preference for the British over the United States Constitution at a stormy meeting of the Georgia Legislature in November, 1860.

Toombs was politician enough not to expose diplomatic secrets publicly, but at Montgomery he must have given reassuring statements *in camera* regarding the attitude of the powers of Europe. The Southern aristocrat, of course, was well aware that the all-important support of the empires of the Old World could not be expected except on the basis of reciprocity. That meant the destruction of the Republic and the erection of a "congenial" system of government in the new Confederacy. Whether or not Toombs himself was directly involved in talks offering the crown of a future confederate kingdom to a European prince cannot be ascertained. But he evidently knew of the negotiations and relied on them. Chevalier Huelsemann, in his report to Foreign Minister Count Rechberg of February 7, 1861, called attention to an obviously inspired article in the "organ of the French government in New York."

The article, to which the Austrian Ambassador attached such importance, was the semiofficial answer to a previous New York *Times* article which "revealed" that "Commissioners of South Carolina and Mississippi" had asked Napoleon III's help for a projected Confederacy as far back as August, 1860, and had "held out to him the perspective of an American crown." Napoleon's answer to the "surprising offer" was noncommittal, according to the *Times*, but "the Emperor shall have declared that 'in the nineteenth century no European government would ever dare to recognize a State based exclusively on slavery.'"

Although details of the *Times* report were called "naïve" by Napoleon's American newspaper, it confirmed "its essential point" and on the basis of its own information felt "authorized to consider as true":

1. That neither in the conferences of August, 1860, nor in those of January, 1861, has there been any question of material encouragement or assistance to be granted to the South by the French government;

2. That the question of the recognition of a Southern Confederation by France has constantly been treated from the viewpoint of *faits accomplis*;

3. That for such an eventuality France had no other obligation to observe than the general rules of current policy adopted by the whole world;

4. That further concrete negotiations were postponed until the time when developments will have clarified the situation;

5. That, finally, the only fact discussed in any particular had been the possibility of a blockade of Southern ports by the naval forces of the North. In this respect the French government declared that its conduct would be ruled by the principles of maritime rights as stipulated by the annex to the Treaty of Paris of 1856.

The French article indicated that negotiations between the plantation aristocracy of the South and Europe's Old Order had begun months before the election of Lincoln—probably right after his nomination as Presidential candidate of the Republican Party. It also showed that after the news leaked out, the French government was anxious to appease the North without alienating the South. As for the offer of an "American crown," this was far less incredible at the time than it is now. Crowns were, indeed, on sale in the last century by and for the *ancien régime,* which used the royal headgear as a lid over the boiling social kettle of republicanism. This was true not only in Europe; the Mexican counterparts of the Southern slaveholders were admittedly seeking a European prince to bring them a golden crown weighted heavily with foreign arms and ammunition.[1]

NAPOLEON'S REMARK that "in the nineteenth century no European government would ever dare to recognize a State based exclusively on slavery" was probably prompted by his ambiguous role as a "liberal" dictator. On the other hand, the Southern commissioners explained to His Majesty, according to the *Times* report, that "the South Carolinians were largely descended from the Huguenots and for this reason they felt a warm admiration of and affection for France as the 'mother country.'"[2] However, the "affection" of the slaveholding descendants of the French Huguenots did not prevent Southern agents from offering the nonexistent crown to an English prince of royal blood also, as claimed by other reports sent by Chevalier Huelsemann to Vienna.[3]

It is difficult to ascertain the extent and the penetration of such offers and negotiations, which were necessarily kept secret and were denied whenever questioned by

[1] J. M. Gutiérrez de Estrada, Mexican monarchist leader, to Prince Richard Metternich, Austrian Ambassador in Paris, July 4, 1861.

[2] Huelsemann to Rechberg, February 7, 1861, Appendix I.

[3] *Ibid.,* Appendix II.

the uninitiated. But reports of Southern agents peddling a crown at the courts of Europe are recurrent in Huelsemann's dispatches to Vienna. Between June 8 and August 7, 1861, he sent four messages containing news items on this subject to Count Rechberg.[4]

Considering the bitterness of Civil War propaganda, Northern accusations against Southern representatives, and vice versa, were often dismissed as unfounded by contemporary historians. Significantly, however, Huelsemann stressed the "authoritative" comment of the French government's newspaper confirming that Southern agents were received by Napoleon III. In a later report the New York *Times* named "young Captain Bonaparte of Baltimore" as the prince who was asked by the Southerners to "accept the position of Military Dictator of the Southern Confederacy, with a crown at his disposal. . . . Fortunately for him," the *Times* added, "Capt. Bonaparte . . . refused the unclean and unnatural proposition." [5]

Captain Jerome Napoleon Bonaparte belonged to the American branch of the French dynasty. He was the grandson of Jerome Bonaparte, the first Napoleon's recalcitrant brother, who defied the Emperor by marrying Elizabeth Patterson, beautiful daughter of a wealthy Baltimore merchant, during his 1803 visit to the United States. The Emperor annulled the American marriage and forced his brother to wed a German princess.

The son of Jerome and Elizabeth, Jerome Napoleon Bonaparte, married Susan Mary Williams, whose father was one of the richest men in Massachusetts. Jerome Napoleon, Jr., their son, born on November 5, 1830, in Baltimore, was educated at West Point, but resigned his American commission to join the army of his second cousin,

[4] Huelsemann to Rechberg, June 8, June 14, July 12, and August 7, 1861.

[5] Huelsemann to Rechberg, July 2, 1861, Appendix.

Napoleon III, in 1854. He was decorated by the Emperor for his "distinguished services" in the Crimean and Italian wars, and it is likely that he played a prominent role in Napoleon's American plans. These plans, however, were not ripe for implementation at the time Captain Bonaparte received the "unclean offer" and he had to decline. Napoleon III wanted no premature conflict with the United States, and Jerome Napoleon, Jr., had good reason to fear the confiscation of his family's American property if he should identify himself with the cabal against Washington. Later developments precluded young Bonaparte from playing a major role in history.

AS TO HOW the news was received in the Southern states, Huelsemann had sent yet another item showing the findings of the London *Times* correspondent after the latter had canvassed the South. It said that the "gentlemen planters" of the seceded states virtually longed for "getting one of the Royal House of England to rule over them."[6] The New York *Times* insisted that the "aristocratic few" had deceived the British correspondent as to the real sentiments of the people in the South and added: "Whenever South Carolina shall swing from her republican moorings, if such a thing shall ever happen, it will be in favor of no scion of European royalty. It will be . . . when some leader of a subsidized soldiery, possessing the energy and will power to wield them, shall grasp by their aid the powers of government and strike down republicanism and make himself a monarch."[7]

A hundred years ago the New York *Times* was not widely read in Europe. Its article made no impression on the imperialist powers, who were already preparing to challenge the Monroe Doctrine and probe the strength of

[6] Huelsemann to Rechberg, February 7, 1861, Appendix III.
[7] Huelsemann to Rechberg, June 14, 1861, Appendix.

republicanism in America. They also were determined to choose their own candidate for each and every available American crown.

IMPERIALISM WAS at its zenith in Europe when the Civil War began, and the time was not yet forgotten when all America was a colony of Europe. The bombardment of Fort Sumter, which opened the hostilities between North and South, was hailed by Europe's rulers as a heavenly signal to regain and redistribute America among themselves. Southern agents, who were treated "confidentially" before, got official invitations after the ominous twelfth of April, 1861. But Mexican royalists beat them to the courts of Europe.

Mexico already had behind her three years of civil war between the aristocratic "Church Party" and the liberal "Constitutionalists." On February 4, 1861, exactly one month before the inauguration of Lincoln, Chevalier Huelsemann reported the complete defeat of the Conservatives, led by the Spanish-Mexican aristocrat, General Miguel Miramón. Washington was quick to recognize the victorious Juárez government which confiscated the large estates, including those of the biggest landowner of Mexico, the Catholic Church. President Juárez, "The Indian," handed the envoys of the Papal States and Spain their passports. Envoys of France and Britain and other European countries had left "voluntarily." [8]

Prominent conservatives fled to Europe and joined some of the earlier émigrés who were already trying to sell the crown of Mexico. Before the revolution of 1848, Gutiérrez de Estrada, one of the most influential Mexican aristocrats, had repeatedly appealed to Chancellor Prince Metternich for help in re-establishing monarchy under a European prince in Mexico. His efforts were subsequently

[8] Huelsemann to Rechberg, February 4, 1861.

23

supported by ex-President General Santa Anna and, after the sweeping victory of the liberals, by Miramón, who had established himself at the court of Queen Isabella of Spain. Miramón's ablest aide, Almonte, went to Napoleon's Paris, and the political Archbishop of Mexico, Labastida, who had been banished by Juárez, joined the Papal Court at Rome. But the most successful among all monarchist exiles was dashing Don José Manuel Hidalgo y Esnaurrizar, much younger and handsomer than his coconspirators, who attached himself to the beautiful and adventurous Empress of France, née Eugénie Montijo of Spain. He became her favorite and she his champion for a monarchistic crusade against America.

III

BESIDES SPLITTING APART THE young Republic, the Civil War rapidly developed into a great historical divide between the social streams of the Old World and the New.

While the *ancien régime* of two continents looked for salvation to the imperial courts, the revolutionaries of Europe threw their moral and physical support behind the Union. Early reports of Lincoln's ambassadors—Charles Francis Adams in London, William L. Dayton in Paris, and John Lothrop Motley in Vienna—commented on the "menacing attitude" of the respective courts and governments but at the same time emphasized that the interventionist plans of the autocratic rulers were "exceedingly unpopular" with the masses. Labor and liberal elements of the European middle classes displayed their sympathy for the Union in public demonstrations and were frequently joined by all opponents of the existing regimes. Nationalists in the Habsburg Empire and anti-Bonapartists in France were equaled and even surpassed in their pro-Union fervor by the textile workers of England—despite the mass unemployment caused by the sudden cessation of cotton shipments from the blockaded South. Public opinion in Europe, although often ruthlessly suppressed, was partly responsible for the cautious attitudes of the imperial governments.

Italian, Hungarian, German, French, Spanish, Polish, and Irish exiles flocked to the banners of Lincoln. Indeed, they had played an important part in the electoral victory of the Midwestern railsplitter, a champion of slaves, refugees, and homesteaders,[1] those land-hungry pioneers who claimed virgin land on the strength of their toil. In 1860, the year of Lincoln's election to the Presidency, there were more than four million foreign-born in the United States, living predominantly in the states which later formed the Union. It may safely be assumed that at least one sixth of the Union population was foreign-born, and the first and second generations of immigrants exceeded the number of citizens of American-born parentage. The greatest number of immigrants at the time came from England, and the next-largest group from Germany. Most of them were imbued with the revolutionary spirit of '48 and were usually led by political émigrés of their native lands.

Lincoln himself was on record as having supported the cause of Kossuth as early as 1848-49. He spoke out in favor of Europe's revolutionaries during his Congressional term. Early in the Civil War he offered to the great Italian leader Garibaldi a command in the Union army. One of Lincoln's stalwarts was Carl Schurz, a leader of Germany's revolutionary youth in 1848, who swung German-American votes to Lincoln in 1860. Schurz, appointed Minister to Spain after the inauguration of Lincoln, returned before the end of the year to join the Union army as brigadier general of volunteers. He was soon commissioned a major

[1] Lincoln's Homestead Act of 1862 gave a quarter section of unoccupied public land to settlers after five years' residence.

general, sharing this high rank with a fellow exile, Franz Sigel, who had been commander-in-chief of the Baden insurrection. United States Brigadier General Ludwig Blenker, another German 48-er, died of wounds in October, 1863.

Brigades and lesser military units formed of German, Irish, Italian, and other nationals were fighting in the Union army. Among the ex-revolutionaries applying for army commissions was the Polish Count Adam Gurowski, who even asked Lincoln for colonelcy of a colored regiment to prove his dedication to the ideal of universal freedom and equality. (The notoriously cantankerous Count's application was declined; instead, he was appointed a translator in the State Department, from which post he was later dismissed.)

Three French princes of the House of Bourbon-Orléans were also among the foreign officers attached to the headquarters of the Army of the Potomac. The Count of Paris, Pretender to the throne of France, the Duke of Chartres, and the Prince of Joinville were playing an ornamental role in the entourage of the Union commander, General George B. McClellan. They never held any post of military importance, but for Lincoln they had a nuisance value in his diplomatic chess game with Napoleon III. For Chevalier Huelsemann, of course, the three princes in the service of the Republic were a source of constant embarrassment. In one of his reports the Austrian Ambassador criticized Lincoln for having too little consideration for "the extreme sensibility of the Emperor of France to courtesies shown to princes of the House of Bourbon." [2]

THE MOST POPULAR and successful of all revolutionary leaders of Europe, Giuseppe Garibaldi, came very close to being invested with a high—if not the highest—command in the Union army. In 1860,

[2] Huelsemann to Rechberg, October 15, 1861.

the year of Lincoln's election, he was at the summit of his fame after having conquered the Kingdom of the Two Sicilies and Naples with his thousand volunteer "Redshirts." True, he had reluctantly renounced his republican ideals and handed over his conquests to King Victor Emmanuel II of Sardinia in order to aid the unification of Italy. But he remained the popular hero of the Risorgimento—the struggle of the Italians to get rid of their medieval princes and foreign domination. He had also fought in the revolutionary armies of Brazil and Uruguay. In 1861 Garibaldi was a name to conjure with on both continents.

Little wonder that disappointment in his own generals and the early defeats of his armies induced Lincoln to consider Garibaldi, who had already expressed his sympathy for the Union cause. Less than a week after the disastrous defeat of the Federals at Bull Run, Secretary of State Seward—obviously upon Lincoln's insructions—entrusted Henry B. Sanford, United States Minister at Brussels, with the task of offering to Garibaldi "the grade of major-general in the army of the United States . . . with the cordial approval of the whole American people." [3]

The rank offered was the highest the President could bestow, and it was widely assumed that Lincoln and his Cabinet were prepared to assign a vital command to Garibaldi. Ambassador Adams in London believed that some American diplomats had offered the Italian leader the opportunity "to take over the supreme command in America." [4] Evidently General McClellan, Commander of the Army of the Potomac, and General Winfield Scott, military head of the United States army, would not have approved. Yet, despite bitter criticism in certain military circles, the most popular general of his time would have

[3] July 27, 1861, National Archives, Washington.
[4] *Proceedings*, Massachusetts Historical Society, 1907–8, referred to by J. G. Randall and R. N. Current in *Lincoln the President*.

been assured of a tremendous welcome in America, which he had frequently called his second home.

Garibaldi himself, when Seward's offer reached him, was in temporary and not quite voluntary retirement. He had found himself far from being satisfied and was in disagreement with his King, who had sent his army to halt Garibaldi's volunteer corps in his campaign against the Papal States. Garibaldi's ambition was thwarted by this compromising attitude of Victor Emmanuel and the King's protector, Emperor Napoleon III. So Garibaldi was quite willing to seek new laurels abroad and was inclined to accept the American proposition. Suddenly, however, the plan was dropped, and Seward withdrew his offer.

One reason for the withdrawal—never fully explained—was indicated by Chevalier Huelsemann in a report to Vienna. The Ambassador of the "Most Catholic Emperor" implied with satisfaction that Lincoln had decided to yield to the power of the Church of Rome. "As for Garibaldi," says the report, "his presence here would have meant one more trouble; it would have had a particularly bad effect upon the Irishmen and the Catholic clergy. Archbishop John Hughes of New York spoke out rather vehemently against this project. . . . "[5]

MINOR DIVERSIONS notwithstanding, the American Civil War accelerated the pace of social change in both hemispheres and clarified the dividing line between conflicting social systems. The situation in its international aspects was reminiscent of the great struggle between revolutionary France and the *ancien régime* of Europe at the end of the eighteenth century. The American Civil War as well as the French Revolution brought forth an international coalition which lined up its forces against the hated adversary, the emergent Republic.

[5] Huelsemann to Rechberg, October 15, 1861.

Revolutionary France, after stamping out its enemies within, took up the challenge of the surrounding monarchies, and the result was Napoleon I. In the case of the United States, the Republic was split in two, and wisdom dictated a policy of temporizing in face of the European challenge. This policy found its expression in Abraham Lincoln.

A slow but profound thinker, one who deliberated each and every action, a champion of tolerance who had immense respect for human life, Lincoln was anything but a born leader of armies. Nonetheless, he was a leader of men, a statesman of clear vision who saw the goal without losing sight of the road that led to it.

Lincoln was a pacifist at heart. He went to the limit in his efforts to avoid civil war, reluctantly offering to the South a *status quo* on the question of slavery. "There will be no bloodshed unless it be forced on the government," he said shortly before Confederate batteries opened fire on April 12, 1861. When the South attacked, he reacted with unexpected energy, but even then he preferred a war of attrition and blockade in order to prevent unnecessary bloodshed.

He was often misunderstood and abused by his contemporaries. His most important general at the beginning of the war, West Pointer George McClellan, was contemptuous and downright arrogant. Lincoln's reaction was characteristic: "I would gladly hold General McClellan's horse for him if he would only win victories." McClellan was eventually removed from command—not for his arrogance, but because he failed to win victories.

Lincoln included in his war Cabinet some of his personal adversaries, both conservatives and radicals. He appointed Edwin M. Stanton, who had publicly criticized him, as Secretary of War, and William H. Seward, his defeated rival for the Republican Presidential nomination, as Secretary of State. It took almost superhuman patience mixed with firmness to mold such diverse elements into an efficient governmental machine.

Exiled leaders of the European revolution showed more understanding of the President of the Union than many of his American associates. Carl Schurz drew a prophetic picture of him when the war President was the target of vicious attacks even within his own camp. "He is an overgrown nature-child and does not understand artifices of speech and attitude," Schurz said. "But he is a man of profound feeling, just and firm principles, and incorruptible integrity. One can always rely on his motives, and the characteristic gift of this people, a sound common sense, is developed in him to a marvelous degree. . . . He is the people personified; that is the secret of his personality. . . . In fifty years, perhaps much sooner, Lincoln's name will stand written upon the honor roll of the American Republic next to that of Washington, and there it will remain for all time." [6]

COMMON SENSE, INDEED, dictated a conservation of the Union's war potential and avoidance of foreign conflicts. Under the pressure of war psychosis, however, common sense often waned even in the best brains of the nation. Intelligent and shrewd politician that he was, William Seward himself was not above being caught in the whirl of war psychosis. Less than a month after Lincoln's inauguration the new Secretary of State formally proposed the adoption of an aggressive policy toward European powers. Obviously trying to discourage interventionist sentiment displayed by the *ancien régime*, Seward told Lincoln: "I would demand explanations from Great Britain and Russia and send agents into Canada, Mexico, and Central America, to raise a vigorous spirit of independence on this continent against European intervention,

[6] Carl Schurz to his friend Theodore Petrasch, October 12, 1864, referred to by Claude M. Fuess in *Carl Schurz, Reformer*.

and, if satisfactory explanations are not received from Spain and France, would convene Congress and declare war against them." [7] Possibly Seward hoped for an upsurge of nationalist feeling in America by a bold challenge to the empires across the sea, but he gravely misjudged the situation.

The maritime powers of Europe were already resolved to take advantage of the American Civil War, and provocative steps on the part of the Union would only have strengthened their hand in favor of intervention on behalf of the South. The leaders of the Confederacy, on the other hand, knew that their ultimate success was dependent on the support of the European empires, whom they regarded as their natural allies. They would, indeed, have welcomed a war between the Union and the empires, but for reasons diametrically opposed to those of Seward.

LINCOLN'S APPRAISAL of the international situation was unclouded by war psychosis or wishful thinking. He quietly shelved Seward's foreign-policy program and substituted his own, based on his simple and prudent maxim of "one war at a time." He stood firm against provocations from abroad as well as hysteria among his own followers, yet—where no fundamental issues were concerned—he always preferred a policy of appeasement to that of challenge and aggression.

One of the earliest diplomatic conflicts between the Union and the empires was the so-called Burlingame Incident, which almost led to the severance of relations between Washington and Vienna.

The sympathy of the United States in general and Lincoln's Republicans in particular for the revolutionaries of Europe was a long-established fact. Chevalier Huelsemann had frequently expressed indignation at the cordiality

[7] Seward's Memorandum to Lincoln, April 1, 1861.

displayed in America toward exiles of the anti-Habsburg revolutions. He never forgot his bitter feud with Daniel Webster over favors shown to Hungary's Kossuth, and he also remembered that Abraham Lincoln, back in the Springfield days, had offered a resolution at a public meeting which called for recognition "in governor Kossuth of Hungary the most worthy and distinguished representative of the cause of civil and religious liberty on the continent of Europe." This, however, had taken place about ten years before when Mr. Lincoln was just a local politician and could be ignored by an envoy of the Emperor. But the righteous ire of the Chevalier rose to the boiling point when President Lincoln, in the first month of his administration, announced the "provocative appointment" of Anson Burlingame, a "violent radical," to the post of Minister Extraordinary at the Court of His Apostolic Majesty Francis Joseph I.[8]

Former Senator Burlingame was guilty of giving moral support to the revolutionary leaders of Europe and, above all, of having sponsored legislation in favor of recognizing the new, anti-Austrian Italy of the Risorgimento. Plainly, such a man could not be allowed to enter the exalted presence of the Emperor. Huelsemann protested and asked patrician Senator Sumner to make this clear to Secretary of State Seward. When this failed, the Austrian envoy objected, remonstrated, and threatened grave consequences, and finally, in a report to Austrian Foreign Minister Count Rechberg, suggested his own recall from Washington.[9] His stubbornness, however, was equaled, if not surpassed, by that of Seward. The Secretary of State rejected all protests of Huelsemann and instructed Burlingame to proceed to Vienna. The Chevalier—after making sure of Count Rechberg's approval—prepared to leave Washington. Burlingame,

[8] Huelsemann to Rechberg, March 22, 1861.
[9] Huelsemann to Rechberg, March 26 and April 5, 1861.

on his arrival in Paris, was informed by Austrian Ambassador Prince Metternich that His American Excellency would not be received by the Emperor.

At this point Lincoln intervened. Tension with Britain was growing, Napoleonic France aligned itself manifestly with the Confederacy, and Lincoln wanted no foreign involvements. He instructed Seward that rupture with Austria must be avoided. On June 14, 1861, Huelsemann triumphantly forwarded to Count Rechberg Seward's telegraphic message informing him that Burlingame "has been commissioned United States Minister to China."

President Lincoln sent a new envoy to Vienna, with a warmly worded letter of credentials addressed to His Imperial Royal Majesty, Francis Joseph I:

Great and Good Friend:

I have made choice of J. Lothrop Motley, one of our most distinguished citizens, to reside near Your Majesty in the quality of Envoy Extraordinary and Minister Plenipotentiary of the United States of America. He is well informed of the relative interests of the two countries and of our sincere desire to cultivate and strengthen the friendship and good correspondence between us; and from a knowledge of his fidelity, probity and good conduct, I have entire confidence that he will render himself acceptable to Your Majesty by his constant endeavors to preserve and advance the interests and happiness of both nations. I therefore request Your Majesty to receive him favorably, and to give full credence to whatever he shall say on the part of the United States; and most of all when he shall assure Your Majesty of their friendship and wishes for your prosperity. And I pray God to have Your Majesty always in His safe and holy keeping.

Written at the City of Washington this fifteenth day of August, Anno Domini, one thousand eight hundred and sixty-one.

Your Good Friend,
ABRAHAM LINCOLN

Motley was accepted by the Emperor and received at court. Burlingame proceeded to the Far East, where the first waves of the Industrial Revolution were beginning to pierce the ancient walls of tradition. He was later extolled as "the most successful diplomat America has ever sent to Eastern lands." [10]

The Burlingame Incident notwithstanding, Lincoln was far more fortunate in the choice of his envoys than in the selection of his generals—at least during the opening phase of the Civil War.

[10] L. M. Sears, *A History of American Foreign Relations.*

IV

WHILE THE STORM IN THE Austrian teacup was abating, thanks to a spoonful of diplomatic sugar administered by Lincoln, heavy hurricane clouds were gathering over the Atlantic.

The courts of London, Paris, and Madrid, anxious to exploit the Civil War for their own purposes, were greatly encouraged by the early military victories of the Confederacy. The Battle of Bull Run proved to them that the Union forces were outgeneraled by the gentleman-warriors of the South. Conveniently overlooked were the lack of boots for the marching armies now threatening Washington itself, an "iron famine" in the Confederacy, and the fact that "there was not a mill in the whole country [South] which could roll a 2½ inch plate." [1]

Outright interventionists in the military and naval

[1] James D. Bulloch, *The Secret Service of the Confederate States in Europe.*

councils of Europe's Atlantic powers gained influence, and joint action in defiance of the Monroe Doctrine was considered. British shipyards—with the connivance of Her Majesty's government—began building cruisers for the Confederacy, and the French general staff drew up secret plans for landing troops in Mexico. Some leaders of the Spanish *ancien régime* envisaged the reconquest of Mexico, and financiers in Paris and London displayed eagerness to launch a loan for the Confederacy.

The ominous clouds over the Atlantic were heavily charged with electricity.

THE FIRST THUNDERBOLT was released by an unpremeditated incident. It brought the Union to the brink of war with England.

The Confederate government sent two new commissioners, John Slidell and James M. Mason, to Paris and London, respectively, to try again for formal recognition of the Confederacy. In the fall of 1861 they ran the Federal blockade to Havana, where they embarked on the British mail steamer *Trent* sailing for Southampton. On November 8, alert Captain Charles Wilkes, commanding the U.S.S. *San Jacinto*, a 15-gun Union steam-sloop, overhauled the unarmed British packet and sent a party aboard to remove Slidell and Mason. Captain Wilkes took them as prisoners of war to Fort Warren, Boston Harbor.

Pent-up emotions exploded on both sides of the Atlantic. Public opinion in the Northern states jubilantly acclaimed Captain Wilkes as a hero, at a time when the Union was in dire need of a war hero after a baleful summer of Confederate victories. The Southern generals, Robert E. Lee and Thomas (Stonewall) Jackson, had caught the fancy of the ecstatic South in search of a new idol and a father image. The North had only the seventy-four-year-old hero of the War of 1812 and the Mexican War, General Winfield Scott, with the appropriate sobriquet of "Old

Fuss and Feathers," and the pompous young would-be-Napoleon, General George B. McClellan, both below comparison with their opposite numbers in the South. Disillusioned Northerners were blaming their generals for lack of initiative and pluck and were happy to find both military virtues in Captain Wilkes, who had snatched the two "traitors" from the hands of their British "protectors."

Moreover, only a few days after Northern warships had begun to blockade Southern ports, the British government had incurred the wrath of the Union by its hurried proclamation of neutrality, thereby giving status to the Confederacy as a belligerent power. This was denounced in Washington as an unfriendly act, indicating British intention to grant full recognition to the Confederate state and to open Britain's markets, dockyards, and vaults to the "rebels."

PRIME MINISTER Lord Palmerston had never concealed his sympathy for the South, and the *Trent* affair gave him a welcome opportunity to humiliate Washington, mobilize the British navy, and send troop reinforcements to Canada. He and his Foreign Secretary, Lord Russell, drafted an aggressive note demanding immediate release of the prisoners and an apology from the United States for violating the British flag.

It is an unresolved question whether Palmerston or Russell was the more bitter opponent of the Union. By descent they both belonged to the highest British aristocracy; by party affiliation they were Whigs. Their powerful position in British political life was based chiefly on their shrewd opportunism and adherence to the political alliance between the Whig segment of the aristocracy and the upper middle class of industrial England. Three decades before the American Civil War, Palmerston had championed the emancipation of slaves in the British possessions, whereas Russell had been one of the backers of the First

Reform Bill which gave franchise to the wealthier middle classes.

Palmerston had been in his late twenties and Russell in his early twenties when, during the War of 1812, United States raiders had virtually destroyed the British merchant marine in the North Atlantic. Experience advised them against taking unnecessary risks, particularly since the Civil War promised to destroy the Republic anyway. They were, however, more than willing to do their bit toward this eagerly desired end, which would eliminate their Atlantic rival and would demolish forever the Union's dangerous influence over Irish revolutionaries and other dissatisfied subjects of the British Crown.

The wearer of the crown, Queen Victoria, was no Union sympathizer either, but she listened to the warning words of the gravely ill Prince Consort. A prince of the House of Saxe-Coburg-Gotha, and a nephew of King Leopold I of Belgium, German-born Prince Albert distrusted Napoleon III, who had hastily offered his help to England and sent an unrequested protest note to Washington backing up Britain against the United States. Two weeks before his death, the Prince Consort exposed himself to criticism of overstepping his constitutional limits and rewrote Palmerston's note, considerably moderating its tone and inviting the explanation that Captain Wilkes's naval exploit had been unauthorized by the Union government.

Under normal circumstances the Prince Consort's attitude would have precipitated another conflict between the Crown and Britain's parliamentary government. But both Palmerston and Russell seem to have curbed their ambition in view of the naval successes of the Union which outweighed the more spectacular but less crippling defeats of the land armies of the North. Port Royal of South Carolina had surrendered to the Federals in November, shortly after Fort Hatteras of North Carolina and other minor forts were taken by Union forces. The improvised blockading navy of the North—which consisted chiefly of hastily bought and armed merchant ships—rapidly tightened its grip and was successively sealing the Atlantic outlets of the Confederacy, one by one.

Moreover, Palmerston, although a professed friend of Napoleon III, could still remember the anti-British aspirations of Napoleon I and was wary of French encouragement. For once he heeded Prince Albert's warnings, which were confirmed by highest diplomatic information. Obviously, Napoleon III was hoping for a British-American war—and not only for the purpose of seeing America humiliated and weakened.

In a cynically forthright report to Vienna, Ambassador Prince Richard Metternich wrote to Foreign Minister Count Rechberg: "The French press—an obedient instrument of the government—campaigns for a war between England and the United States. . . . What conclusion could be drawn, but that Emperor Napoleon . . . has some secret motive for seeing his rival engaged in an enterprise of long duration. Seemingly his plan would be to remain neutral at the beginning of the war, but . . . he is likely to take advantage of a favorable opportunity for active involvement. . . . Naturally, Napoleon would not let England alone seize all the honors, profits, and moral prestige which might be gained from this war."

Speaking for his own country, Metternich pointed out the "advantages" that might be derived for the benefit of Austria. "On the one hand," he said, "the English and the American armies would absorb adventurers and mercenaries ready to serve any cause—men like those who have constituted the backbone of Garibaldi. On the other hand, attention of the disillusioned public, such as in Italy, would be focused on the grandiose spectacle of the new strife."

Metternich advised a wait-and-see policy for the Austrian Empire with regard to the Civil War.

Another passage in the Prince's report illuminates the high aristocracy's views of the *Trent* incident. Metternich claimed that "the gravity of Captain Wilkes's conduct" was not appreciated in the United States. Americans, he said, "are seeing it only as a slap given to a power which for many years has been humiliated by its old colonies by all kinds of insolent rebuffs." [2]

Humiliation was the very thing Lord Palmerston could not take. He prided himself on having enhanced British prestige all over the world, and prestige and power were for him synonymous. The violation of the British flag had to be redressed, and therefore the question of war or peace in the Atlantic depended ultimately on the American answer to the British note.

War hysteria gripped a large part of the Union, and the overwhelming majority of Lincoln's Cabinet dared not oppose the public outcry for the rejection of the note. Secretary of the Navy Welles officially commended Captain Wilkes, and the House of Representatives voted its approval of the capture of the Confederate commissioners. Lincoln, however, recognized the dangers. The President defied Congress and overruled his Cabinet members. By a timely publication of Napoleon's diplomatic intervention he cooled off anti-British sentiment and, with a master stroke worthy of Britain's divide-and-rule tradition, he settled the explosive *Trent* affair. Lincoln—by that time fully supported by Seward—appeased Her Majesty's government by surrendering Slidell and Mason to the British. At the same time a face-saving, vigorous rejection of the French note supporting the demands of London was sent to Paris.

IN ONE OF HIS typical unbiased reports sent to Rechberg about this time, Huelsemann makes only a passing reference to the *Trent* affair:

[2] Prince Metternich to Count Rechberg, December 22, 1861.

My Lord:

The first action of the rebel Congress at Richmond was the Resolution to transfer the seat of the government of the Confederate states to Nashville, the capital of Tennessee. This city is more centrally located than Richmond, which would require the presence of a strong army as a protection against attack. Apparently, Mr. Davis—having realized that the threat against Washington implied by making Richmond his capital did not produce the desired result—finds a voluntary retreat preferable to an enforced change of residence under the pressure of events. The naval expeditions are menacing all the Atlantic states of the South; and Virginia, exhausted as it is by the presence of three hundred thousand men—the two armies [North and South]—for four months, will have its communications with the two Carolinas disrupted from the sea and the coastal roads.

The Federal government has taken another measure, severe and destructive to the maritime interests of the South: they have sent some forty old ships, loaded with stones, to be scuttled at the entrances of the ports of Charleston, Savannah, and probably other ports of the Gulf. This damage will have to be repaired after the war by very expensive operations. The government has an immense advantage over the enemy in its navy and the inexhaustible man power offered by New England and New York. By contrast, the states of the South have no vessels nor can they have any, because the social class which furnishes sailors to the North consists of slaves in the South, and the slaves would abandon the ships entrusted to them at the first opportunity offered.

Mr. Davis and his partisans doubtless imagined that England and France would use the first pretext to assure the permanent destruction of the Union, and at present they still count on the consequences of the arrest of Mr. Slidell and Mr. Mason aboard a British steamship. Southern confidence in the power of cotton was exaggerated; and although they could prolong the war, they have not the means of long resisting the vast resources of the North which are being mobilized for their destruction on land and sea. A foreign war would change the situation and offer a chance of different results.

The affair of Captain Wilkes is in *status quo*. The sheet enclosed herewith contains details of his reception in Boston.

The most important internal question for the administration is that of slavery, affected as this institution is by the Civil War. The President and half the Cabinet are in favor of the principles of the Constitution which sustain slavery; the others more or less favor emancipation. The President's system assures him a great following in the Central states, yet weakens his position in New England. The restitution of the Union and of peace seems possible when adopting the views of the President; however, should he not arrive at making them prevail in his administration and in the Congress, the Civil War would be infinitely prolonged, one might say, and the part the slaves are likely to play in it would fill the cup of sorrow of the states of the South to the brim.

Please permit me, my Count, to tender my profound respect,

Hülsemann

To avoid a fratricidal war, Lincoln was, indeed, willing to let slavery linger on in the South. He was convinced that slavery was doomed to extinction anyway.

Austria's role in the *Trent* affair was predetermined by the cautious attitude of the imperial government. Professing only an interest in maintaining world peace, Count Rechberg instructed his envoys in Washington, Paris, and London to indicate Vienna's willingness to act as mediator in the dispute. Although Austria's good offices were not invoked, Seward expressed the President's appreciation in a letter to Chevalier Huelsemann dated January 9, 1862:

Sir:

I have submitted to the President the note you left with me which was addressed to you on the 18th of December last by Count Rechberg, touching the affair of the capture and detention of the British contract steamer *Trent* by Captain Wilkes of the *San Jacinto*.

I send you a copy of the correspondence which has passed on that exciting subject between this Government & the Governments of Great Britain and France, and I have to request that you will transmit these papers to Count Rechberg.

The Imperial Royal Government will learn from them two important facts, namely,—first, that the United States are not only incapable for a moment of seeking to disturb the peace of the world, but are deliberately just and friendly in their intercourse with all foreign nations; and secondly, that they will not be unfaithful to their traditions and policy as an advocate of the broadest liberality in the application of the principles of international law to the conduct of maritime warfare.

The United States, thus faithful to their sentiments and while at the same time careful of their political constitution, will sincerely rejoice if the occasion which has given rise to this correspondence shall be improved so as to obtain a revision of the law of nations which will render more definite and certain the rights and obligations of States in time of war.

I shall esteem it a favor, Sir, if you will charge yourself with the care of expressing these sentiments to your Government, and will at the same time assure Count Rechberg that the President appreciates very highly the frankness and cordiality which the Government of Austria has practised on an occasion of such great interest to the welfare of the United States.

I avail myself of the circumstance to offer to you, Sir, renewed assurances of my very high consideration.

William H. Seward

Seward's interest in a revision of the law of nations reflected, of course, the fact that the United States was a blockading power severing the Atlantic line of commerce and contraband for the Confederacy. At the time, however, the Imperial government showed no interest in maritime warfare.

SCARCELY HAD LINCOLN weathered the first Atlantic hurricane when a second storm, much wider in scope and potentialities, swept over the ocean. On October 31, 1861, the "London Conference" launched a joint naval action of Britain, France, and Spain against the United States-supported Republic of Mexico. The tripartite expedition was diplomatically described as a debt-collecting mission, and the high contracting parties announced in advance that they were not seeking any territorial gains. But the Conference was preceded by years of Mexican royalist intrigues at the courts of Europe, and by the fall of 1861 the French-sponsored candidacy of an Austrian prince for the Mexican throne was already a widely discussed "secret" in the capitals of the world.

For appearances' sake, the three European naval powers had even invited the United States to join their intended "seizure of Mexican customhouses." But to Count Muelinen, who was in charge of the Austrian Embassy in Paris during the absence of Prince Metternich, Napoleon's Foreign Minister Count Alexander Walewski admitted that the invitation was a "pure formality." He added that "the Union is in a state of dissolution and could therefore under no circumstances participate in the naval expedition." [8]

Lincoln and Seward had no illusions about the true intentions of the European "debt collectors." It was evident that the expedition was aimed at nothing less than the overthrow of the republican regime in Mexico. It was equally evident that a Mexican monarchy, supported by Europe's empires, would be a natural ally of the Confederacy and a permanent danger to the Union. Lincoln was also fully aware of the inability of his navy—which had no capital ships to spare—to prevent a landing at Veracruz. He knew that war with the three European powers would be a suicidal undertaking.

At home Lincoln again was confronted with war hysteria and with Seward advocating action against Europe's powers. But again Lincoln stood his ground: he stuck to

[8] Count Egon Caesar Corti, *Maximilian and Charlotte of Mexico.*

his dilatory tactics and hoped for an early breakup of the Tripartite Alliance. He was soon vindicated.

THE BRITISH, FRENCH, and Spanish fleets were, in accordance with the London Conference, supposed to arrive simultaneously in Mexican waters and jointly occupy the customhouses of Veracruz. Madrid, however, instructed the Governor General of Cuba to embark hurriedly 6,000 colonial troops and dispatch them to Mexico. So the Spanish landings took place on December 17, 1861, three weeks before the arrival of the first British and French troopships.

The Spanish expeditionary force was commanded by General Count Juan Prim, who had a wealthy Mexican wife and a burning ambition to become the Spanish Viceroy of reconquered Mexico. The commander of the French contingent—at the beginning there were only twenty-six hundred troops, but they were being rapidly reinforced— was Vice-Admiral Jean Pierre Edmond Jurien de la Gravière, who was secretly instructed to contact and support the conservatives and royalists of Mexico.[4] Both Prim and de la Gravière were authorized by their respective governments to advance into the interior, whereas the British Commander Admiral Dunlop—who had only eight hundred troops at his disposal—had orders not to proceed beyond the coastal region.

Within a few weeks, the jealousies, suspicions, and rivalries inherent in the tripartite expedition began to hamper its progress. Lincoln now agreed to issue a serious warning to the European powers, anticipating conflicting reactions in the various capitals and increasing discord among the Tripartite Allies. The note, signed by Secretary Seward, was addressed to Ambassador Dayton at Napoleon's court. It is the only American document of which more

[4] French Foreign Minister Edouard A. Thouvenel to Admiral Jurien de la Gravière, November 11, 1861.

than one copy was kept in the Austrian Imperial Archives. Evidently great importance was attributed to it and it was studied by Francis Joseph as well as by his brother Maximilian and the imperial ministers.

Washington, 3ᵈ March 1862

Sir,

We observe indications of a growing opinion in Europe, that the demonstrations, which are being made by Spanish, French and British forces against Mexico, are likely to be attended with a revolution in that country, which will bring in a monarchical government there, in which the crown will be assumed by some foreign Prince.

This country is deeply concerned in the peace of nations, and aims to be loyal at the same time in all its relations, as well to the allies as to Mexico. The President has therefore instructed me to submit his views on the new aspect of affairs to the parties concerned. He has relied upon the assurances given to this government by the allies, that they were seeking no political objects, and only a redress of grievances. He does not doubt the sincerity of the Allies and his confidence in their good faith, if it could be shaken, would be reinspired by explanations apparently made in their behalf, that the governments of Spain, France and Great Britain are not intending to intervene and will not intervene to effect a change in the constitutional form of government, now existing in Mexico, or to produce any political change there in opposition to the will of the Mexican people. Indeed he understands the allies to be unanimous in declaring that the proposed revolution in Mexico is moved only by Mexican citizens now in Europe.

The President, however, deems it his duty to express to the Allies, in all candor and frankness, the opinion that no monarchical government, which could be founded in Mexico, in the presence of foreign navies and armies in the waters and upon the soil of Mexico, would have any prospect of security or permanence. Secondly, that the instability of such a monarchy there, would be enhanced, if the throne should be assigned to any person not of Mexican nativity. That under such circumstances the new government must speedily fall, unless it could draw into its support European alliances, which, relating back to the first invasion would in fact make it the beginning of a permanent policy of armed European monarchical intervention, injurious and practically hostile to the most general system of government on the continent of America, and this would be the beginning rather than the ending of revolution in Mexico.

These views are grounded upon some knowledge of the political sentiments and habits of society in America.

In such a case, it is not to be doubted, that the permanent interests and sympathies of this country would be with the other American republics. It is not intended on this occasion to predict the course of events, which might happen as a consequence of the proceeding contemplated, either on this continent or in Europe.

It is sufficient to say, that, in the President's opinion, the emancipation of this continent from European control, has been the principal feature in its history during the last century. It is not probable that a revolution in a contrary direction would be successful in an immediately succeeding century, while population in America is so rapidly increasing, resources so rapidly developing, and Society so steadily forming itself upon principles of Democratic American government. Nor is it necessary to suggest to the allies the improbability that European nations could steadily agree upon a policy favorable to such a counter revolution, as one conducive to their own interests, or to suggest that however studiously the allies may act to avoid lending the aid of their land & naval forces to domestic revolutions in Mexico, the result would nevertheless be traceable to the presence of those forces there, although for a different purpose, since it may be deemed certain that but for their presence there, no such revolution could probably have been attempted or even conceived.

The Senate of the United States has not indeed given its official sanction to the precise measures, which the President has proposed for lending our aid to the existing government of Mexico, with the approval of the Allies, to relieve it of its present embarassments [sic.] This however is only a question of domestic administration. It would be very erroneous to regard such a disagreement as indicating any serious difference of opinion in this government, or among the American people, in their cordial good wishes for the safety, welfare & stability of the republican system of government in that country.

I am, Sir

Your obedient servant,
WILLIAM H. SEWARD

This was plain talk, an undisguised threat of support for the Republic of Mexico as well as the antimonarchist revolutions in Europe. Lincoln and Seward—without delving into the complex nature of the historical forces designated retrospectively as the Industrial Revolution—identified themselves with the eighteenth- and nineteenth-century revolutions and defied the counterrevolution of the European emperors and, by implication, that of the Mexican feudalists and Southern slaveholders.

THE UNION GOVERNMENT'S warning was underlined by a series of Federal victories during the first months of 1862. Ambassador Adams, in London, made the most of the improved situation, and Lord Palmerston was said to have remarked that he was not willing to pull out the chestnuts for Napoleon. After all, the basic rule of Britain's foreign policy was expressed in Palmerston's own maxim that "Britain has no permanent friends or enemies, but merely permanent interests." Early in April, 1862, Britain withdrew from the tripartite enterprise, and frightened Spain followed suit.

But the Atlantic storm had not yet spent its fury. It gathered new strength as Napoleon III launched his conquest of Mexico to establish there a puppet empire with a Habsburg as its nominal head. When Britain and Spain withdrew, the Emperor of the French lost two meddling allies, but he was to acquire a new one, his fellow Emperor Francis Joseph I, whose backing promised to enhance his dynastic prestige, disguise his imperialistic aims, and assure him the active support of the *ancien régime* of both continents as well as the blessing of the Pope.

"Emperor Napoleon sees in the monarchic solution [of the Mexican problem] a chance to promote civilization," said a Metternich report, "and the Empress is enthusiastic." [5]

Lincoln's statesmanship faced another, perhaps its most severe, test.

[5] Metternich to Chargé d'Affaires Count Rudolf von Muelinen, October 12, 1861, for transmission to the imperial government.

V NAPOLEON III, THE AMBI-
tious weakling, had a reliev-
ing sense of humor. It was a cynical humor but, vain as he
was, he did not spare himself. Defending his political vacil-
lations, he once referred to the alternating pressures brought
upon him by the members of his inner circle. Closest to
his heart and his ears, the Emperor indicated, were his wife
Empress Eugénie, his half brother the Duke of Morny, and
his faithful friend and Minister of Interior Count Persigny.
His own inconsistencies, explained the Emperor, reflected
the conflicting views of his closest advisers. "The Empress," he said, "is a legitimist [extreme conservative,
Bourbonist], Morny is an Orléanist, I am a republican.
There is only one Bonapartist in my inner circle, Persigny
—and he is crazy." [1]

Indeed, it was Empress Eugénie who was responsible

[1] Octave Aubry, *The Second Empire*.

for the most fateful of Napoleon's inconsistencies which had a direct bearing on the social conflicts in America. For it was she who induced the French Emperor to make peace with his archenemy, Emperor Francis Joseph I of Austria, at the expense of his Italian ally. And it was Eugénie who persuaded her husband to exploit the American Civil War, support the Confederacy, and send a large army to Mexico. Finally, it was due chiefly to Eugénie's influence that Napoleon offered the Crown of Mexico to Francis Joseph's younger brother, Archduke Ferdinand Maximilian, to seal the bond between the two Catholic empires of Europe.

NAPOLEON III WAS NOT entirely a stranger to America. He had come to the United States as Prince Louis Napoleon Bonaparte after his unsuccessful attempt at a military coup at Strasbourg in 1836. The French government had let him off with the comparatively light sentence of banishment and put him aboard a ship sailing for America. The exiled Prince was pampered by New York society hostesses during the season of 1836–37, and his flagging self-confidence was inflated by the flattery of snobs. As a result he gained a distorted picture of the social and political trends in the United States and was led to believe that the Bonapartist cause enjoyed a wide popularity in America.

He apparently had obtained more encouragement from his wealthy American relatives than from his cousins in Europe, who showed little faith in a Bonapartist restoration. Jerome Bonaparte's American offspring (from his marriage with Elizabeth Patterson of Baltimore) were admirers of Louis, whereas Jerome's children from his second marriage (to Princess Catherine of Wuerttemberg) were jealous of their adventurous cousin. Both Prince Jerome (Plon-Plon) Bonaparte and his sister Princess Mathilde of the Wuerttemberg branch failed to identify themselves with Louis's "cause" until the latter moved to the Elysée Palace as elected President of France. Then Jerome was appointed to a number of high positions, and Mathilde accepted her cousin's invitation to be his hostess at the Palace. But Louis Napoleon's marriage to Eugénie revived the old jealousies, probably because Mathilde had hoped to become Empress of France herself, and Jerome felt himself deprived of his unofficial status as Crown Prince of the Second Empire.

BEAUTIFUL, RESOLUTE, ambitious Eugénie had an inferiority complex as big as the Palace of Versailles, owing to her relatively humble origin, aggravated by her foreign ancestry. True, her father was a Spanish aristocrat, the undistinguished Count of Montijo and Duke of Peneranda. But her mother was the daughter of a Málaga innkeeper, an adventurous Scotsman of the Kirkpatrick clan, who—after a detour to America—had settled in southern Spain and made a sizable fortune by catering to drunken sailors, soldiers, and itinerant noblemen. Through his newly acquired wealth and connections, the jovial innkeeper climbed to the social rank of a titular United States consul at Málaga.

The noblest of Bill Kirkpatrick's customers, as far as titles went, was the one-eyed, elderly Count of Montijo, who late in life inherited a ducal title and was a wine- and women-loving adventurer, not unlike his Scotch-American-Spanish host. In his younger years Count Montijo had joined the Grand Army of Napoleon I and, after the collapse of the First Empire, had returned to his Spanish homeland. The aging warrior fell in love with the young and pretty daughter of the shrewd Kirkpatrick and married her, causing a minor upheaval among the grandees of Spain.

Her father's liquid and solid gold and her husband's titles, however, overcame social prejudice, and the Montijos kept open house for friends of the aging Count, particularly for Bonapartists, old and young.

Their second daughter, Eugénie, a blue-eyed, auburn-haired, self-willed charmer, met Prince Louis Napoleon before his *coup d'état* and knew how to hold his affection. Nevertheless, striving to imitate his great uncle, Napoleon "the Little" tried to contract a political marriage, but none of the old Catholic dynasties was willing to let him have an authentic royal princess. So he returned to Eugénie and married her on January 29, 1853, only two months after he had proclaimed himself Emperor of France.

Socially, Eugénie was somewhere between the two wives of Napoleon I—Josephine de Beauharnais, the gay adventuress, and Marie Louise, daughter of the Austrian Emperor. Politically, however, the Spanish-Scottish Empress of the French towered far above both of her predecessors. Napoleon I had brooked no interference from his wives in affairs of state, whereas Napoleon III welcomed Eugénie's interest in politics for two reasons: first, he expected to make good use of her designing mind and feminine charms, and later he wished to deflect her attention from his rapidly increasing amorous adventures.[2]

Napoleon set an example in licentiousness to the subjects of his Second Empire. His liaisons were numerous, as were his illegitimate progeny. He used to jest that he had to make good for his five and a half years of solitude in the grim Fortress of Ham where he was sent under sentence of life imprisonment after his second miscarried coup in 1840. This was another of his habitual exaggerations. In Ham Louis Napoleon became the father of two sons of a pretty girl who took care of his laundry and other mundane needs.

THE MOST SERIOUS of Napoleon's liaisons had a political background. His favorite was

[2] Publication of "Secret Memoirs" concerning Napoleon's love-life was suppressed in Vienna after an exchange of confidential diplomatic notes between the French and Austrian Foreign Ministries.

the "incomparably beautiful" Italian Countess Virginia di Castiglione, described by hostile Princess Pauline Metternich, wife of the Austrian Ambassador, as "Venus descended from Mount Olympus." [3] The red-blonde, green-eyed beauty had the body of a "nymph sculptured of pink marble," commented the Austrian Princess with unusual generosity—although it was well known to her that the goddess was a secret diplomatic agent from the enemy camp. Both Eugénie and Napoleon were also aware of the Countess's mission, which fact increased the Empress's jealousy but failed to diminish the Emperor's infatuation.

Eugénie took a broad view of her imperial husband's infidelities, but she hated the Countess. The Italian beauty was more than a rival for the affection of her husband or an object of art in his extensive *collection d'amour*. She was a political adversary, sent to the royal bedchamber by the shrewd Count Camillo di Cavour, architect of Italian unity, who had secured the alliance of Napoleon III against Austria in the late 1850's.

With Napoleon's military backing, Cavour had succeeded in uniting most of Italy under King Victor Emmanuel II of Sardinia. Only Venetia was still under Austrian rule, and the Pope clung tenaciously to his temporal domain, Rome and the Papal States. Cavour saw with misgiving Napoleon's attempts at *rapprochement* with the conservative powers of Europe which obstructed the way to complete unification of his country. He was fully alive to the goings on in Napoleon's inner circle, and was resolved to oppose Eugénie's influence on the Emperor and to win back the French monarch for Italy. Cavour entrusted this all-important task to the most beautiful woman of his country, who was "commissioned" to capture the old roué's heart and regain France's military support. Countess Castiglione, so gossip claimed, was quite willing to make the sacrifice—for the sake of Italy, of course.

[3] Princess Pauline Metternich, *Éclairs du Passé*.

The patriotic fervor of her husband, Count François di Castiglione, equaled hers. After having squandered his fortune on the Countess in the first two years of their marriage, the Count had entered King Victor Emmanuel's personal service. He became his King's equerry and she His Majesty's favorite. The young couple separated but both swore allegiance to the same monarch.

Cavour, the greatest patriot of all, was passionately attached to the Countess but loyal to his King. By solving his dilemma, he proved his statesmanship. He enrolled the beautiful Countess in the diplomatic corps of Piedmont-Sardinia and sent her to Paris. "I asked the lovely Countess," said Cavour in an intimate letter to his friend Luigi Cibrario, "to flirt with—and, if necessary, to seduce—the Emperor." Thus the temptress was removed from the court of Turin, and yet she was royally rewarded with an honorable status, a high income, and an exalted assignment—all to the glory of the Fatherland.

The Countess's success at the gay and brilliant court of the Second Empire was overwhelming. Her radiant and well-subsidized beauty conquered fashionable Paris and became the focal attraction of the magnificent gala receptions at the Tuileries. Napoleon the connoisseur succumbed to her charms at first sight, and Eugénie raged. The inner circle became divided more than ever, and the "Italianissimi" (friends of a united Italy) won new supporters in and outside the Cabinet.

For two or three years Cavour had excellent reason to be proud of his Countess, who, he claimed, was his distant cousin and not-so-distant lady friend. As for the moral side of the affair, Cavour is quoted by his biographers: "If we did for ourselves what we do for our country, what rascals we should be."

But Eugénie's complexes were shaped and intensified by her jealousy. To compensate for her lack of royal ancestors she had become a champion of the *ancien régime*.

Now she upheld the cause of Austria and the Church of Rome in the imperial councils and raised vehement objections to a further unification of Italy. She challenged Cavour and his lovely agent and, in the long run, won the race with the "goddess."

EMPRESS EUGÉNIE and Bull Run —the eloquence of a jealous woman and the initial victory of the Southern generals—united Napoleon's inner circle on a common ground. They were split on almost every other question and approached the problem of transatlantic intervention from widely divergent points of view.

Napoleon's half-brother Charles Auguste, the Duke of Morny, was of multiple royal descent and was called "king of rakes" in Paris, a title he fully deserved. Illegitimate son of Queen Hortense, mother of Napoleon III, Morny's father was the Count of Flahaut—a general of Napoleon I —who had traced his own illegitimate descent to King Louis XV. Gay Queen Hortense, née de Beauharnais, was the daughter by a previous marriage of Josephine, first wife of Napoleon I. The Emperor had married off his stepdaughter to his brother Louis, whom he later appointed King of Holland.

The Duke of Morny surpassed his half brother as a spendthrift and a libertine. He was an inveterate gambler and a confirmed corruptionist, and financed his fantastic extravagance by no less fantastic operations on the stock exchange and by selling his political influence to the highest bidder.

For Morny, sending an expeditionary force to Mexico was a gigantic financial operation. The Duke was a "confidential" business partner of a reckless Swiss financier, J. B. Jecker, who came to the rescue of the last conservative Mexican government by advancing General Miramón 3,750,000 francs against 2,000 per cent interest. This was in 1859, shortly before the victory of Juárez's republican

57

forces over Miramón. It was evident that the 75,000,000 francs in Mexican bonds given by Miramón to the magnanimous Swiss banker would be valueless, unless collected by force. Switzerland, of course, had no navy or army to speak of, so Jecker set his hope on France and the Duke of Morny. For a 33 per cent participation in the profits, Morny granted French citizenship to Herr Jecker and threw his half-brotherly influence in the scales for armed intervention in America. And since the Confederacy needed ships and ammunition and cash, Morny had just the right connections to help out the gentlemen of the South.

Jean Gilbert, Count (later Duke) of Persigny, was no moralist either. But his principal motive in approving the plan of intervention was to strengthen the Second Empire by a new military success abroad which might appease the growing opposition at home. He had seen this scheme work before. It was Persigny who had urged French military intervention in Italy against Austria, and he had been one of the staunchest advocates of France's participation in the Crimean War against Russia. He distrusted the Habsburgs and the temporal power of the Church. But, above all, he distrusted his own Parisians, as evidenced by his instruction to Baron Haussmann, famous prefect and rebuilder of Paris. He bade Haussmann replace the cobblestones of the boulevards with asphalt, which could not be used by potential demonstrators as missiles against the police.

For once, the inner circle showed a unity in purpose although diversity in design. Members of the Cabinet and the High Command quickly followed suit. Feverish conspiratorial activity began, which is reflected in the correspondence of Their Majesties, Their Highnesses, and Their Excellencies of Paris, London, Brussels, and Vienna, with ramifications in Madrid, St. Petersburg, and Rome. Emperor Napoleon III was pulling the strings of this gigantic intrigue, while Empress Eugénie was pulling the strings of the Emperor.

Eugénie's growing political influence was pointedly described by Count Rudolf von Muelinen, Chargé d'Affaires of the Austrian Embassy in Paris during the absence of the Ambassador, Prince Metternich. The highly confidential report was written on October 18, 1862, after the Palace victory of Empress Eugénie, who, supported by Minister of State Count Alexander Walewski, forced Napoleon's only pro-Union, pro-Cavour, and anti-"Papist" Foreign Minister, Edouard Antoine Thouvenel, to resign from the Cabinet:

Paris, October 18, 1862

SECRET

My Lord!

There is but one opinion in the camp of the Papists, to celebrate the skill of Count Walewski in conducting the campaign which has just been ended with the ascent of M. Drouyn de Lhuys to a position of power. The Count of Bourqueney, who is competent to judge the question, has assured me that he [Walewski] surpassed himself and that the strength of his convictions together with his courage and loyalty were the deciding factor in winning the just cause. The former Ambassador of France in Vienna [Count of Bourqueney] could not find enough praise to point out the adroitness and selflessness of the Minister of State in the face of severe criticism and accusations.

If one gives his due to the champion who has helped justice and religion to triumph over demagoguery and socialism, how much more one has to admire the August Consort of the French Sovereign who by her persistent and generous efforts has defeated the designs of the Italianissimi. *It is Empress Eugénie who, during her sojourn at Biarritz, has carefully prepared the change we have just witnessed. With an intense perseverance possessed only by women to such a high degree, she has influenced the mind of her husband, keeping him on a pitch of explosive mood, adroitly availing herself of*

*the good instincts that occasionally are exhibited by Napoleon.
I recall that she really exerted great influence on the decisions
of the Emperor and it is to be hoped that this splendid result will last long enough to produce happy consequences.*
[Italics are the author's.]

Allied with Count Walewski and supported by Countess
Walewska, the Empress has pursued her aim with the aid of
M. de la Gueronnière's pen, whose newspaper "la France,"
founded under the moral guidance of His Majesty, has power-
fully contributed to the change of public opinion. It also neutralized the detestable semiofficial press which, with the help
of Count Persigny, had become an organ of Italy and, unin-
tentionally, the instrument of the revolution [against the Austrian Empire] and which took advantage of this domestic
question to promote its ultimate ends.

And now this courageous trio is supported by an energetic statesman of strong character and well-known convictions, who is absolutely able to carry on a fight and bear the
whole burden. With the emergence of this ally, who was able
to make his own conditions when he accepted the Cabinet
appointment, it is possible to hope the Emperor's policy will
take a more favorable turn; although it would be an illusion
to expect palpable results from one day to the other, it is likely
that the *status quo* will be firmly maintained toward and
against all. The touchstone will be the circular instructions of
the new Foreign Minister to the Emperor's diplomatic agents
abroad. I have been assured that M. Drouyn de Lhuys will
confirm that never under any pretext will the Emperor evacu-
ate Rome or deliver the Capital of Christianity to the im-
petuousness and greed of Italy. If this is to be the case an important point would have been gained, but I believe that it
might provoke bitter opposition in the Council and possibly
the resignation of M. de Persigny.

The result of the wrangle confirms that Count Walewski
has lent his support to M. Drouyn de Lhuys in a loyal and disin-
terested way. My sources have recently confirmed to me my assumption—which I had the honor of repeatedly expressing to
your Excellency—that the State Minister had thought of accepting the portfolio of foreign affairs himself or entrusting it tem-

porarily to Prince de Latour d'Auvergne, with the expectation of later being called to succeed him. A man like M. Drouyn de Lhuys, on the other hand, is not likely to leave his position unless the policy followed by him and Count Walewski would once more be abandoned by the Emperor. The State Minister, however, recognized the vanity of these considerations and decided to approve the candidacy of M. Drouyn de Lhuys, thus abandoning his personal interest. From this moment on, his power doubled, his activity trebled, and the goal was reached.

Ending my humble report, I take the liberty of pointing out that Count Walewski, in warning me of an approaching danger now hovering on the horizon, has given evidence of his foresight, his knowledge of the situation, and his ability to size up correctly his own strength. Sizing up his strength might explain his ardent desire to have Prince Metternich at his side since the Prince's influence on the Emperor is well known to him. I am inclined to believe that the repeated hints of the State Minister about the desirability of the return of the Prince [to Paris] should be partly attributed to the Empress, who attaches great importance to the co-operation of the Imperial Ambassador.

It is fortunate that the victory has been obtained without the assistance of Prince Metternich, since his presence in France would have provided a weapon to the Italianissimi, who are always inclined to speak of the political interference of Austria and would not have failed to attribute the latest events to pressure on the part of the Ambassador. In one of my interviews with Count Walewski, I took the liberty of calling his attention to those facts, which, however, he did not admit at the time for fear of a possible reverse. Yet I am sure he, nevertheless, realizes that my remark was true and well founded.

Please accept, My Lord, my profound respect,

Muelinen

Count Alexander Walewski had a singular standing in the Second Empire. He was the illegitimate offspring of the storied love affair of Napoleon I and the beautiful Polish Countess Maria Walewska. Alexander was recognized as the son of Napoleon the Great and was for a while close to Napoleon the Little. His position at the imperial court, however, was modified by the traditional triangle which played such an important role in French imperial-royal politics. His wife, the fiery Countess Poniatowska-Walewska, was one of the mistresses of Napoleon III, and Count Alexander became (quite logically) confidant of Eugénie.

The all-important Foreign Ministry was turned over to Count Walewski's friend, Drouyn de Lhuys, a "Papist," pro-Austrian, and pro-Confederate politician of the Second Empire.

In urging the return of Prince Metternich to Paris, Muelinen could not be unaware of a sarcastic bon mot of the time claiming that Empress Eugénie was the Ambassadress of conservative France to Prince Metternich of Austria.[4]

Tall, handsome, blond-bearded Prince Metternich's co-operation was invited by Eugénie not only against Cavour's Italy but also against the North American giant and Mexico. She detested the United States as a "hotbed of republicanism" and repeatedly expressed the opinion that "sooner or later we shall have to declare war on America."[5] She spoke disparagingly of Lincoln and was greatly amused by hostile caricatures of the American President. "Why is the French-American scientist Du Chaillu searching Africa for the missing link when a specimen was brought from the American backwoods to Washington?" This gibe at Lincoln's expense evoked much merriment among the ladies of the Tuileries.

Eugénie greeted the outbreak of the Civil War as a godsend which opened the gates for European intervention on behalf of the feudalists of the Confederacy and the royalists of Mexico. It was, she insisted, a great oppor-

[4] Octave Aubry, *The Second Empire*, and John Bigelow, *Retrospections*.

[5] Henry Salomon, *L'Ambassade de Richard Metternich à Paris*.

tunity to gain more power and glory for imperial France and her dynasty. (What a compensation for her "foreigner" complex!) It enabled Napoleon to offer the Mexican Crown to a prince of the House of Habsburg as a gesture of conciliation with a view to a close alliance. (What a humiliation for Cavour and his Countess!) And she envisioned a crusade of the three Emperors, Napoleon, Francis Joseph, and Maximilian, to restore monarchy and the power of the Church—first in Mexico and later in the remnants of the disintegrating United States. (What an opportunity to awe the liberal-republican opposition in France!)

Such were her arguments which persuaded Napoleon to send his armies to Mexico and his "goddess" back to Italy.

VI

EMPEROR FRANCIS JOSEPH I was suspicious by nature and cautious by experience. His ambassadors' reports on Confederate and Mexican emissaries offering two new crowns to Napoleon III evoked mixed emotions in his imperial bosom. Scion of one of the oldest dynasties of the world, the Austrian Emperor regarded the American republics as an iconoclast conspiracy against the world order he represented by the grace of God. Therefore, the idea of restoring the monarchic system in North America was welcome to him. But he detested Napoleon and suspected his motives.

Nevertheless, Francis Joseph could see Prince Metternich's point that it would be unwise to decline Napoleon's gesture of *rapprochement* and his proposal to put an American crown on the head of a Habsburg archduke. The Austrian Emperor had little interest in the Confederate states, but Mexico was a different matter. Had it not been one of the brightest jewels in the crown of Charles

V, his great ancestor upon whose realm the sun never set? And had not Spain and the vanquished Aztec Empire once been ruled by the House of Habsburg? [1]

As for Napoleon, the obnoxious upstart must be given credit for showing moderation at the Italian peace negotiations and for restoring the monarchy in France and trying to do the same in America. Also, there was a precedent for coming to terms with the Napoleons. Francis Joseph had a bureaucrat's predilection for precedents, and he recalled that his illustrious grandfather, Emperor Francis I, after having been defeated six times by Napoleon I, had given his daughter Marie Louise in marriage to the victorious French conqueror. It was Prince Clemens Metternich, dominating figure of the Holy Alliance, who had been the adviser of his grandfather on the family and political alliance with Napoleon I. And now, half a century later, Clemens's son, Prince Richard Metternich, was advising an alliance with Napoleon III.

Of course, history may repeat situations but it does not duplicate events. Francis Joseph had no marriageable daughter, and Napoleon III was in the firm hands of his Empress Eugénie. There was no danger of the new Napoleon proposing to a Habsburg Archduchess.The idea of giving away his younger brother by granting him permission to accept the Crown of Mexico proffered by the French ruler seemed to the Austrian Emperor much less disturbing—particularly since handsome and talented Ferdinand Maximilian was Francis Joseph's successful rival for popularity in the multilingual Austrian Empire.

FERDINAND MAXIMILIAN was only two years younger than Francis Joseph, but in their political and social views they were a century apart. The

[1] Charles V, son of Philip I and Joanna of Castile, was Emperor of the gigantic Habsburg realm in the 16th century (1519–1558) and, as Charles I, King of Spain (1516–1556).

young Archduke believed in a liberal, constitutional monarchy and insisted that the highest duty of a ruler was to improve the lot of his subjects. In contrast, Francis Joseph was immersed in the eighteenth-century ideas of dynastic glory and claimed that it was the first duty of his subjects to worship and obey their Emperor.

His unruly people disagreed with him, of course, and so did his charming, young, liberal-minded wife, Empress Elizabeth. But his subjects who dared to defy him were either executed or thrown into prison, whereas Elizabeth was kept out of politics by the powerful alliance of her mother-in-law and the Emperor. A former Bavarian princess, Elizabeth soon conformed to the rigid rules of the House of Habsburg; she withdrew from politics and later also from marital life. She spent much time in traveling and became eventually an innocent victim of a Habsburg-hating political assassin.

Within the imperial family, Archduke Ferdinand Maximilian was the only one who ventured to raise his voice against the oppressive autocracy of the first decade of his brother's reign. He criticized the police state, the military "pacification" of the rebellious nationalities, the severity of justice, and the almost inhumanly rigid court discipline. He quickly gained popularity, and his name was acclaimed even when sullen crowds silently demonstrated against the pompous public appearances of Francis Joseph. But Max, as he was called by his intimates, was soon shown his place by his elder brother—and this place was calculatedly far from Vienna. When the Mexican Crown emerged on the horizon, the Archduke was a commander of a second-rate fleet in the Adriatic, spied upon by his subordinates.

Ferdinand Maximilian and Princess Charlotte, daughter of the King of Belgium, were married on July 27, 1857, at Brussels. As a sort of wedding present, he was given the Vice-Royalty of Lombardy and Venetia by Francis Joseph, but his powers were limited and lasted for only a brief period. Otherwise, he was Commander of the Austrian navy and sent on various missions abroad.

He had many friends, but none who could really understand his tantalizing ambitions frustrated by his second-born status. And there were none to whom he could fully entrust his rebellious thoughts—none but his young wife Charlotte. Although theirs was a marriage of convenience, arranged by Charlotte's father, King Leopold I of Belgium, and Francis Joseph, she became passionately attached to Maximilian and shared his aspirations and complexes. The blond, blue-eyed, slightly effeminate poet-prince became the star of her world stage, to whom she gave the cues, whispered the missing lines, and provided the applause. She was as energetic as he was mild, her dark beauty contrasted strikingly with his fair complexion, and her burning brown eyes disclosed an almost masculine will power—and incipient madness.

She saw her adored star—and willed him—in the role of a ruler, an emperor. When Francis Joseph sent his Minister, Count Rechberg, with Napoleon's proposal to Miramar, the secluded dream-castle built by Ferdinand Maximilian on the shore of the Adriatic, the Archduke was more than receptive. Indeed, he was imbued with the idea that he was chosen by Providence to take the monarchic principle to deviating America, to uplift the suffering people of Mexico, and to add new luster and humaneness to majesty.

AT THE END OF 1861, when President Lincoln complied with Lord Palmerston's demands in the *Trent* incident and diplomatically ignored the tripartite "debt-collecting" expedition to Mexico, the imperial intrigues at the European courts reached the stage of a conspiracy against republican America.

All three principals in the imperial conspiracy agreed

that the supreme aim of their joint offensive was the destruction of the bulwark of republicanism and the reintroduction of the blessings of monarchy in North America. As a personal benefit, Napoleon hoped to gain new revenues and marital peace. Francis Joseph hoped to restore his prestige and get rid of his popular brother. Ferdinand Maximilian hoped for glory and for deliverance from the irksome tutelage of Francis Joseph.

All three were anxious to obtain the co-operation, or at least the benevolent neutrality, of the other powers of Europe—especially of Britain. This task was entrusted to foxy old Leopold I, uncle-by-marriage of Queen Victoria. Although one of the lesser monarchs, Leopold enjoyed high esteem among the crowned heads of Europe. A German prince of the House of Saxe-Coburg-Gotha, Leopold was chosen King of Belgium in 1831, and displayed extraordinary talents as an administrator and a matchmaker. Among others, he was responsible for the marriage of Victoria with his nephew, Prince Albert, which union strengthened immeasurably his ties with the British Crown.

Leopold was consulted and he expressed hope for eventual British backing of the proposed French-Austrian venture in North America. In a letter to Ferdinand Maximilian, which was duly submitted to Emperor Francis Joseph, Leopold encouraged his son-in-law and, in his circumspect way, indicated his support and approval:

Augsburg, October 25, 1861

My dear Son,

I read with great interest the documents you transmitted to me. It was highly important and necessary for me to learn *your* viewpoint, since, if you had declined the matter as too difficult a task, all further steps would have become superfluous. The matter is of a difficult nature, because of the political demoralization, i.e., the lack of all loyalty and reliability [of the Mexicans] due to a constant change of authority. Two elements have not been quite destroyed, the large estates and the influence of the Clergy. The Indians are not an evil element and are better than the Creoles, although in the cities a part of the Leperos [Indian city-proletariat] may have become bad enough.

If England were following a farsighted policy, she would have a double incentive for supporting this project: first, to see Mexico productive once again; and, second, *to raise a barrier against the United States and provide a support for the monarchical-aristocratic principle in the Southern states.* [Italics are the author's.] Unfortunately, since the reform there are many influences obstructing a policy of real consequence, and discouraging old ministers from initiating such if it might cause personal trouble for them. They [the British Cabinet] are reluctant to pledge publicly their support for an expedition implying intervention in the internal affairs [of Mexico], in order to establish a certain form of government. Should, however, Mexico *herself* choose monarchy, they would recognize the new form of state.

We face the question: Will the Conservatives [of Mexico] have the courage to undertake the necessary steps? They might be encouraged by the approaching help of Europe. On the other hand, I heard that the mob might massacre the Conservatives should it be faced with such an expedition. *Thus, the ultimate decision depends on what the country* ITSELF *would do,* since then we may have firm ground under our feet. Until these developments have taken place, it might be necessary to maintain *freedom of action.* Whether you should abandon your position in Austria in case of a favorable turn of events is a question that none but you alone can answer; unfortunately it cannot be denied that the beautiful monarchy is sick; whether you are able to contribute to its preservation can only be decided by you.

At the time the independence of the Spanish colony was recognized by England, Mexico was a country excellently suited for a monarchy. Some Mexicans of influence had proposed to Canning [George Canning, British Foreign Minister] that he persuade me to take over its government. England,

69

however, was afraid that all-out support [of this proposal] would appear too self-interested and might be dangerous to Victoria. Thus the idea is not new.

The elements of a political life exist in Mexico. Had the secession not taken place in the United States, Mexico would have been seriously threatened from that quarter, since the idea of entirely absorbing her had taken firm root in the United States; but irrespective of the outcome of the war, there can be no longer any thought of further conquest south of the border. On the other hand, the South, as I said before, has an interest in the reorganization of Mexico.

So let us recapitulate: 1) Mexico must herself enunciate the principle. 2) Until this happens, you must insist on your *freedom of action* without, however, declining the offer. 3) France is in favor of it. Spain is *not*. [The Queen of Spain wanted a Spanish prince on the Mexican throne.] Yet they cannot propose a Bourbon to Emperor Napoleon. Moreover, this would be regarded by the Creoles as a complete restoration, which they would not welcome. England will recognize the situation proclaimed by the majority of the Mexicans. Perhaps they will gradually realize that it will be of importance for the state of affairs in the North of America. [For some reason King Leopold switched from German to English in this last sentence.]

Charlotte gave me a well-rounded report of the situation; it could be a fine state if only Heaven were pleased to give guidance for the best. I shall dispatch today my message and hope that you are well. I am still coughing from the catarrh I caught in Wiesbaden.

And now, good-by, I will keep you informed of whatever I can learn, as ever, my dear son,

Your faithful father,
LEOPOLD REX

Leopold, in pointing out that the European powers, by establishing an empire in Mexico, would "raise a barrier against the United States and provide a support for the monarchical-aristocratic principle in the Southern states," put into clear focus the ultimate political aim of the conspiracy. He gave a fairly accurate picture of the European situation which confronted the new Conquistador, Archduke Ferdinand Maximilian. As he had already promised his daughter Charlotte, the King indicated he would undertake "further steps," chiefly to obtain the endorsement of the British government. He, of course, had the ear of Queen Victoria and Prince Albert, but political reforms in England were obstructing the freedom of action of the "old ministers."

Leopold hinted how in his opinion Mexico should "choose monarchy." The conservatives of Mexico "might be encouraged by the approaching help of Europe," but "the mob might massacre the conservatives" if they undertook "the necessary steps." The obvious course would be to protect the conservative minority by a European army of occupation—and until then Maximilian should maintain his "freedom of action." This is exactly what happened.

The letter of the King of Belgium undoubtedly hastened the final decision of Francis Joseph I and Ferdinand Maximilian, who, at a meeting on New Year's Eve in Venice, agreed to accept Napoleon's offer. They shared the French Emperor's view that the Confederacy had become a natural ally and that the Union was no longer in a position to interfere with a monarchist expedition to Mexico. The secret memo on this meeting stated: "In the political respect: should Europe recognize the South as an independent State, we must demand—on a reciprocal basis—that the South should respect the integrity and independence of Mexico." [2] This would have meant the repudiation of the Monroe Doctrine by the Confederacy.

ON THE SAME DAY that he received the first favorable response to his proposal from Vienna, October 9, 1861, Napoleon dispatched a letter to Count

[2] Maximilian's Memo of his meeting with Francis Joseph, December 31, 1861.

Flahaut. General Count Auguste Charles Flahaut de la Billarderie was Napoleon's Ambassador in London and had been a most intimate intimate of the Bonaparte family for many years. Because the dashing aide-de-camp of Napoleon I had been in his younger days a paramour of Napoleon III's mother, Queen Hortense, and father of the Duke of Morny, Napoleon III's half brother, he was referred to by the inner circle as *le Père* and was held in high esteem by the Emperor.

Flahaut was instructed by the Emperor to win Palmerston's support for the conspiracy and to assist the efforts of King Leopold at the court of Queen Victoria on behalf of Archduke Ferdinand Maximilian. Napoleon proposed understanding and "common action" to Britain and continued:

"There is no need for me to enlarge upon the common interest which we in Europe have in seeing Mexico pacified . . . if it were regenerated it would form an impassable barrier to the encroachments of North America. . . . The American war has made it impossible for the United States to interfere in the matter, and what is more, the outrages committed by the Mexican government have provided England, Spain and France with a legitimate motive for interference in Mexico. . . . According to the information I have received, as soon as the squadrons [of the three powers] arrive off Veracruz, a considerable party in Mexico is prepared to seize the supreme power, summon a national assembly, and proclaim the monarchy. . . . I put forward the name of Archduke Maximilian. . . . The Prince's personal qualities, his connection through his wife with the King of the Belgians, who forms a natural link between France and England, and the fact that he belongs to a great nonmaritime power appeared to me to meet all desirable conditions."

Napoleon could not resist flattering his own vanity by adding: "For my part, I confess, I thought it was in good taste for me to propose as candidate (under certain conditions) a Prince belonging to a dynasty with which I had recently been at war."

THE STRATEGY of the emperors, intent on recovering America for the monarchic principle, soon crystallized into a blueprint for gradual conquest: (1) The occupation of Mexico for the new imperial regime; (2) overt financial and moral—and clandestine military—support of the Confederacy; (3) recognition of the Confederate states at an opportune moment; (4) gradual re-introduction of the monarchic system of government into a divided United States; (5) suppression of all republican regimes and revolutions in the New World.

Active intervention in the Civil War depended, of course, on the third step in the general strategy of the emperors. Recognition of the Confederacy would be the hinge on which the fate of North America would turn. European statesmen were carefully weighing the pros and cons in the timing of this step, which would amount to a declaration of war on the Union.

True, the first step was already a violation of the Monroe Doctrine, but then it was camouflaged as a debt-collecting move against the defaulting Republic of Mexico. The second step could also be camouflaged so as to leave the door open for diplomatic negotiations. But the third step constituted a point of no return and therefore had to be meticulously prepared.

The trend of thought of the royal conspirators is reflected in a later letter of King Leopold to his son-in-law.[3] Leopold writes about his attempts to overcome the "timidity" of certain British circles still afraid of the power of the United States. He reports "progress" and advises the following procedure to extend recognition to the South in a devious way: "The form would be a British-French of-

[3] October 27, 1862.

fer of good offices [to Washington and Richmond] possibly with the co-operation of Russia. Should these good offices be declined by the Union, which is likely to happen, the logical result would be the recognition of the Southern states. This also is the opinion of Lord Palmerston."

Eugénie and Napoleon, Francis Joseph and Ferdinand Maximilian agreed in principle, but they all hoped that the occupation of Washington by Confederate forces—their most sanguine expectations seemed to be justified at the time—would induce Britain to consent to immediate recognition.

WHEN CONFEDERATE Commissioner John Slidell arrived in Paris—after the harrowing *Trent* incident—he was received by the Emperor himself and was assured of the eagerness of the imperial government to support the South. Simultaneously Mexico's Hidalgo was informed by the Empress of the plans for the occupation of Mexico by a French army to install an Austrian Emperor for the benefit of the Mexican royalists. Preparations for the recolonization of America had begun.

VII

DURING THE YEAR OF 1862, Washington was repeatedly threatened by the armies of Lee and Jackson and, for a critical twenty-four hours, by the Confederate ironclad *Virginia*. Generals McClellan, McDowell, Pope, Halleck, and Burnside were successively beaten by the far superior strategists of the South in the mountains west of the Shenandoah Valley, at Front Royal, at Winchester, at Port Republic, at Fair Oaks, in the Seven Days' battles, at Slaughter Mountain, at Gainesville and at Second Bull Run. And in September the Confederates crossed the Potomac and invaded Maryland. The advance on outflanked Washington was halted by the Federals at Antietam. The Confederates retired, but in December Lee defeated the reorganized Army of the Potomac at Fredericksburg.

Against this brilliant military record of the Confederacy in the main theater of war between the two capitals,

Washington and Richmond, Union victories faded into insignificance—particularly when transmitted by diplomatic reports to the governments of Europe. Yet those victories were far from negligible. The battle of Shiloh in Tennessee opened the way for a successful invasion of the Southwest by the Union armies, and the capture of New Orleans by a Federal naval expedition wrested the control of that important seaport from the Confederacy. Moreover, the two victorious operations also marked the emergence of two promising military leaders on the Union side. The battle of Shiloh brought General Ulysses S. Grant to Lincoln's attention, whereas the lightning conquest of New Orleans projected Admiral David G. Farragut into prominence.

The recapture of Norfolk by Union forces ended the one-day glory of the Confederate "navy's" threat to Washington. The Confederates had succeeded in raising the scuttled Union frigate *Merrimac* from the waters of Norfolk harbor and, with the help of quickly assembled iron plates, had converted her into an ironclad. She was renamed *Virginia* and, flying the Confederate flag, she sailed up Chesapeake Bay destroying all wooden ships which attempted to block her way to the entrance of the Potomac. Washington was in an uproar, with the Cabinet in emergency session, when a scarcely completed experimental navy craft, the U.S.S. *Monitor*, was steaming down Chesapeake Bay to meet the *Virginia*. The *Monitor*, an ironclad with a revolving turret designed by the Swedish engineer Ericsson, chased the *Virginia* back to Norfolk. Two months later the *Merrimac-Virginia* was blown up by the Confederates as they were abandoning Norfolk and their rebuilt ironclad.

The battle of the ironclads made naval history and heralded the conquest of the seas by the steel vessels of the machine age. Yet it failed to impress Their Majesties and

Their Excellencies who eagerly anticipated the fall of Washington to the armies of the South.

THROUGHOUT 1862 and the first half of 1863, European recognition of the Confederacy and the danger of intervention against the North loomed large over the Atlantic. Recognition would precipitate war with the Union—Secretary of State Seward had said so in unmistakable terms—but the fall of Washington might cause the secession of the border states and perhaps mutiny in the ranks of Lincoln's armies. This speculation induced even the cautious Foreign Secretary of the British government, Earl Russell, to prepare secretly for recognition of the South. From Russell's letters to Palmerston it is evident that the Foreign Secretary played a brilliant game of diplomatic duplicity.[1] On the one hand, he assured Ambassador Adams of the peaceful and correct attitude of Her Majesty's government and officially refused to receive Adams's rival, Confederate Commissioner James Murray Mason. On the other hand, Earl Russell did meet with Commissioner Mason privately and tried, undercover, to promote a European coalition in favor of the Confederacy; without ever publicly revealing his true policy, he urged, *in camera*, recognition of the South by the British Cabinet.

Also, Earl Russell, together with Lord Palmerston, encouraged the construction of war vessels for the South in British shipyards and tacitly permitted these secretly armed ships to "escape" from their docks and hoist the Confederate flag. Indeed, the creation of a Confederate navy to combat the rapidly growing naval forces of the Union was one of the prime concerns of the British government. Chiefly through its agent in Britain, Captain James D. Bulloch, the Confederacy—which had no shipbuilding facilities at home —acquired about 30 vessels, among them the famous cruiser *Alabama*, which alone destroyed some 70 United States

[1] Spencer Walpole, *Life of Lord John Russell.*

77

merchant ships.[2] But the United States navy grew far too rapidly for British comfort. At the beginning of the Civil War the Union navy had only 42 ships in commission, whereas early in 1862 it had 300. Before the war ended, the United States boasted more than 650 vessels and 50,000 sailing men.

The naval strength of the Union was obviously the principal deterrent of war from the British point of view. Nevertheless, Earl Russell was willing to take the risk after the Confederate victories in the summer of 1862. All he was waiting for was the capture of Washington.

THIS EVENT WAS ALSO anticipated in Paris and Vienna. Napoleon III went further than Her British Majesty's government. In July, 1862—almost simultaneously with Lord Russell's covert activities in favor of recognition of the South—the Emperor received Confederate Commissioner John Slidell in audience at Vichy. At a very cordial conference he expressed his willingness to recognize the Confederacy, provided England would agree to co-operate. Three months later Napoleon gave another audience to Slidell at Saint-Cloud, where he revealed his plan to propose a six months' armistice to the belligerents. This coincided strangely with the advice of shrewd King Leopold to his son-in-law Archduke Ferdinand Maximilian, that should "a British-French offer of good offices" be "declined by the Union, which is likely to happen, the logical result would be the recognition of the Southern states." Napoleon also indicated the desirability of the capture of Washington, and suggested building Confederate ironclads in French shipyards.[3]

Slidell and his wife and two daughters were presented

[2] James D. Bulloch, *The Secret Service of the Confederate States in Europe.*

[3] Confederate Commissioner John Slidell to Judah P. Benjamin, Secretary of State of the Confederacy, July 25, 1862. Official Records of the Union and Confederate Navies.

to the Empress and invited to the gala receptions at the Napoleonic court. Soon they developed into regular courtiers; Slidell became an intimate gambling companion of the Duke of Morny and Count Persigny, both closest to the imperial throne, and his pretty daughters married aristocrats. One son-in-law of Slidell belonged to the new financial aristocracy; he was the son of Baron d'Erlanger, banker to Morny and, of course, to the Confederacy. His second son-in-law was Count of Saint-Romain, a legitimate member of the *ancien régime*.

Slidell acquired a fifteen-million-dollar loan for the Confederacy—at terms extremely favorable to Erlanger—and a sort of family membership in the highest of high society of Paris. He soon struck up friendship with the Mexican royalists at the time favored by high society—in particular with the noblemen J. M. Gutiérrez de Estrada and José Manuel Hidalgo y Esnaurrizar. Gutiérrez had been Mexican Ambassador to the court of Vienna, where he married an Austrian countess—reason enough to be sent as confidential envoy to Francis Joseph and Ferdinand Maximilian to support the schemes of the French imperial couple. And Hidalgo was the favorite of Empress Eugénie—reason enough for the Confederate envoy to seek his friendship.

SLIDELL WAS QUICK to realize the significance of the invasion of Mexico for the Confederacy. Evidently, the reintroduction of "the monarchic-aristocratic principle" in North America did not bother him at all, and he was glad to report to Richmond that the future Emperor of Mexico urged France and Britain to recognize the South. Indeed, Maximilian was later to declare that the cause of royalist Mexico and that of the Confederacy were identical.[4] Through his friends Slidell was kept informed of all important developments, and he welcomed

[4] Slidell to Benjamin, December 3, 1863. Official Records of the Union and Confederate Navies.

the royal conspiracy as the best way to ensure permanent imperial backing for the South. His enthusiasm was perhaps dampened but not subdued by such Napoleonic designs as the creation of an "independent" buffer state out of Texas—to gain another French protectorate.

Slidell was realistic enough to see that France's and even more so Britain's willingness to risk a direct conflict with the North depended on the fortunes of war. Washington did not fall, despite the efforts of Lee, who risked the safety of Richmond by weakening its defense forces in order to strengthen his offensive thrust against the North. Aware of the international consequences of an eventual conquest of Washington, Lee explained his strategy simply by saying he was ready to "swap queens." But Lincoln was not willing to gamble and insisted on adequate defense of his capital even though some of his generals were anxious to draw on the capital's reserves. After Lee's advance was stopped at Antietam, Lord John Russell gave up his secret maneuvering for recognition of the Confederacy and, complying with Seward's demand, ordered the seizure of the powerful commerce raiders under construction for the South in the Liverpool docks.

NOT SO NAPOLEON: his and Empress Eugénie's flamboyant Mexican schemes involved France deeply in American affairs. The Emperor se siderable reinforcements overseas, and more were w for embarkation. Co-operation of the Austrian Empire was already a *fait accompli*, and the Mexican royalists and Southern feudalists were negotiating an alliance. The French treasury was depleted, and the opposition had to be appeased by prospects of foreign conquests and a new source of revenue. The Mexican prospects were bright. The new Mexican Empire was to be a *de facto* dependency of France, since it was under the control of the French army of occupation. And within this dependency Napoleon was to establish a sort of crown colony by "leasing" the rich province of Sonora from Mexico. Incidentally, it was Southern-born ex-Senator Gwin of California who called Napoleon's attention to the allegedly rich gold, silver, and iron deposits in Sonora and proposed its joint exploitation.

In order to promote Napoleon's plan to make Texas a buffer state, his emissaries encouraged Texas' double secessionists, who, after secession from the Union, wanted to secede from the Confederacy. Despite the great secrecy surrounding this delicate Napoleonic intrigue, the conspiracy within the conspiracy was discovered, and Chevalier Huelsemann in Washington shook his head in bewilderment. On January 20, 1863, he reported to Count Rechberg. "The imprudent ardor to foment a revolution in Texas against Mr. Jefferson Davis" had got "the French consuls in Galveston and in Richmond" into trouble with the Confederate government. He compared the incident with the "intrigues against the Union government" which had previously called forth serious measures against "Count Mejean, French Consul at New Orleans." The Chevalier found "these odd proceedings of the French diplomatic agents difficult to defend," despite the close co-operation between France and Austria in Mexico. He added with glee that the French Ambassador "M. Mercier will find in the above incident one more reason for taking a leave of absence and returning to France."

Both the Sonora colony and the Texas protectorate were, however, stillborn projects of the Napoleonic mind. Mexican guerrilla warfare was not conducive to capital investments, and, politically, even Maximilian disapproved of French exploitation of Sonora which, he felt, would invite the accusation that he was selling a part of his new empire to a foreign power. Texas, on the other hand, in 1863 lost by death its strongest personality around whom the double secessionists could gather. Samuel Houston, picturesque hero of Texas' anti-Mexican revolution and the first President of the Texas Republic (back in 1836), was Governor of Texas when the Civil War broke out. He refused to join the Confederacy, and the pro-Davis forces removed him from office in March, 1861. His considerable following remained leaderless.

THE OPPOSITION TO Napoleon's policy was strong—and not only among labor, republicans, liberals, and Bourbonists. One of the most prominent lawyers of Paris, professor in the College of France and advocate in the imperial court of Paris, Edouard Laboulaye, who would have been expected to support the imperial government, wrote in a widely circulated pamphlet:

"The commercial interests of France counsel neutrality. This is the surest and speediest means of terminating the war. The political interests of France enjoin her to remain faithful to the great traditions of Louis XVI and of Napoleon. The unity and independence of America, that is to say of the sole maritime power that counterpoises England, constitutes for all Europe the only guarantee of the liberty of the seas and the peace of the world. . . . Are we, out of affection for slavery, after the duration of eighty years, to break the only alliance which never cost us a sacrifice, and never caused us a regret? " [5]

Slavery was generally condemned in Europe, and Lincoln's Emancipation Proclamation greatly strengthened the opposition to the pro-Confederacy policy of the imperial-royal governments. In England popular demonstrations and meetings were held, hailing Lincoln as the "liberator," and pro-Northern manifestations were upsetting the police in France and in other Continental states. The British government yielded, at least on the surface, and surrounded its foreign policy with even more than its wonted secrecy. But Napoleon could not and would not modify his attitude,

[5] *The United States and France, 1862.* White Collection of Pamphlets, Cornell University Library.

which was now committed to the building of a French Empire in America. The still victorious Southern armies were his potential allies, whereas the North was his strongest adversary. He was not unduly worried about the apparent moderation of the British government's attitude. Napoleon counted on the strong dynastic ties between the British monarch and the House of Habsburg, in particular Archduke Ferdinand Maximilian, whose wife Charlotte was a cousin of Queen Victoria.

NAPOLEON SEIZED THE initiative which was relinquished by Earl Russell, and late in 1862—soon after he had replaced his anti-Habsburg Foreign Minister Thouvenel with Eugénie's choice, Drouyn de Lhuys—France officially proposed joint mediation to Britain and Russia. Napoleon's proposal called for a six months' armistice between the North and the South and was calculated to lead to formal recognition of the Confederacy.

The proposal was politely but promptly turned down. Alexander II, Czar of All the Russians, was a dissenter. In opposition to his own *ancien régime*, he instituted liberal reforms; above all he had abolished serfdom at the very time the Civil War had broken out in America. Moreover, he still resented British-French intervention in favor of Turkey, which had led to the Crimean War. The Czar's Foreign Minister, Prince Gorchakov, announced, even before the presentation of France's proposal, that Russia would never join in a plan of interference in the Civil War.[6] A year later—not before the fortunes of war had decisively changed in favor of the Union—Russia sent two fleets, one to New York and the other to San Francisco, as a demonstration of friendship.

The British answer to the French proposal, sent in

[6] Prince Gorchakov to Chargé d'Affaires Bayard Taylor. Verbal statement reported to the U. S. State Department in October, 1862.

November, 1862, said in effect that mediation would have no chance of success. It was also pointed out, with implied irony, that "Her Majesty's government have not been informed up to the present time that the Russian government have agreed to co-operate with England and France on this occasion." [7]

Austria, although insisting that she was not a maritime power and was therefore not directly involved, showed extraordinary interest. Her Foreign Minister instructed his envoys at the respective capitals to report on the situation.

Count Wimpffen reported from London on November 15, 1862, that the British government definitely declined to intervene, and that it was believed Napoleon's principal motive in making the proposal was to obtain a "free hand in Mexico."

From St. Petersburg, on November 18, 1862, Count Revertera informed his Foreign Minister, Count Rechberg, that Prince Gorchakov assured the French Ambassador of his intention to instruct the Russian Minister at Washington, Edouard de Stoeckl, to join the intended "*démarche* of France and Britain in case there is a chance of favorable reception on the part of the Union government." Naturally, such a chance never existed.

Chevalier Huelsemann in Washington pointed out, in his December 10, 1862, report to Count Rechberg, that the French *démarche* is "positively hostile to the United States and favors the South." He expressed belief that domestic policies and the Mexican adventure had induced Napoleon to undertake his *démarche*, "the failure of which must have been anticipated in Paris." Maybe, he added, Napoleon was right, but "it seems to be prudent for other governments not to provoke for nothing the hatred of the United States."

Finally, Prince Metternich in Paris—who completely

[7] Lord Russell to French Minister Drouyn De Lhuys, November 13, 1862.

84

ignored the existence of the United States until the outbreak of the Civil War—sent a number of dispatches on the *démarche* in November and December. Perhaps the most interesting is his letter on the receipt of the news of General Lee's victory at Fredericksburg: "The reverses of the Union army," reported Metternich, on December 30, 1862, "give M. Drouyn de Lhuys an opportunity to renew his *démarche*," which was declined by London.

METTERNICH WAS CORRECT. The next month, January, 1863, Drouyn de Lhuys sent a direct *démarche* to Washington, offering France's mediation to the United States government. The result was a blunt rejection by Seward, supported by a Congressional resolution denouncing foreign interference in the strongest terms.

Once more Napoleon made a rather awkward effort to obtain British co-operation for a new attempt at mediation. In June, 1863, when French troops entered Mexico City and the Confederacy was still undefeated, Napoleon received in private audience two pro-Southern Englishmen. They were John A. Roebuck, an ultraconservative M.P., and his associate, William S. Lindsay, a representative of Britain's powerful shipbuilding industry. After their return to London, Roebuck introduced a resolution in the House of Commons urging the recognition of the Confederacy and disclosing confidential details of his talk with the Emperor of the French. Napoleon issued a denial of Roebuck's statements, which had irritated the British government. For a hundred years, historians have debated the question: Who was the liar, Roebuck or the Emperor? The Austrian Ambassador to Paris gives the answer in his report to Count Rechberg on the audience at Fontainebleau:

Paris, July 1, 1863

My Lord,

The rumors spread by the press about a new French *démarche* submitted to the London Cabinet concerning the recognition of the Southern states of America are taking on a certain consistency. I think I am in a position to inform Your Excellency on the latest development on this question.

Mr. Roebuck and Mr. Lindsay came directly to Fontainebleau in order to ask the Emperor whether it was true that His Majesty would no longer interfere in the affairs of America. The Emperor—as is his custom—allowed himself to be somewhat carried away and to say more on this subject, perhaps, than he wanted to. Indeed Mr. Roebuck said, at yesterday's session of Commons, that Emperor Napoleon had authorized him to reveal to the House that instructions had been given to [London Ambassador] Baron Gros to propose negotiations aiming at the recognition of the South and that His Majesty had complained to him that a confidential communication made to England last fall concerning mediation in America had been shown to Mr. Seward.

M. Drouyn de Lhuys has not concealed from me his despair over the indiscretion committed by his Master. He confided to me that far from having authorized Mr. Gros to submit a new proposal, he had instructed him to maintain a strictly reserved attitude, because he did not want England to take advantage of a new French *démarche* to the American government and benefit by the United States' refusal.

All Mr. Gros has been authorized to do is to reaffirm the facts and to declare that France would not object to any proposal of this kind should it be considered by England.

Accept, my Lord, the expression of my respect.

METTERNICH

That episode—and a series of Northern victories—put an end to all European attempts at direct intervention in the Civil War.

VIII

SUMMER, 1863, WAS THE turning point of the war. The battle of Gettysburg marked the end of Lee's supposed invincibility, the Confederate army was in full retreat, and Grant's Federals took Vicksburg. The Union gained complete control of the Mississippi by capturing Port Hudson, and the Confederacy was split in two.

All these events took place within the first nine days of July. The losses were high on both sides. But the superiority of the North in men and matériel permitted quick replacements, whereas the South scraped the bottom of its barrel of reserves and General Lee suggested the enlistment of Negroes.

Most European statesmen and diplomats, however, were still under the spell of the Confederate victories at Chancellorsville and Fredericksburg. Napoleon's armies entered Mexico City in June, and soon his agents rounded up leaders of Mexico's aristocracy to proclaim the Empire and formally offer the Crown to Archduke Ferdinand Maximilian.

Ambassador John Lothrop Motley reported to Seward from Vienna on September 22nd that "it is, I believe, unquestionable that the Archduke is most desirous to go forth on the adventure. . . . The matter is a very serious and menacing one to us."

A few months before, Napoleon had authorized the construction of four ironclads for the Confederacy and proposed anew mediation between North and South, which would have involved recognition of the Davis government. Little wonder that the leaders of the South—after a reappraisal of the situation—now pinned their hopes on the rising Mexican Empire and on the French armies deployed south of their border.

The importance of Mexico had prompted various attempts at *rapprochement* on the part of the Confederate government even before the French invasion. The military adventurer Colonel John T. Pickett of Kentucky had been sent by Toombs, when he was Secretary of State, to the liberal President Juárez with offers of treaties of friendship and trade. But Colonel Pickett was suspected of conservative sympathies and was not received by Juárez. The high-sounding territorial and financial concessions he offered to other members of the Juárez Cabinet were not taken seriously, particularly since his dispatches to Toombs, defaming the Mexican government, were regularly intercepted.

An imperial Mexico, however, actively supported by the two great powers, France and Austria, was a different matter. Both the economic systems and the political outlook of the *ancien régime* of the two neighbors were essentially related. Confederate slavery and Mexican peonage, the interests of the large plantation owners in the

Southern states and those of the feudal aristocracy in Mexico, bore a close resemblance.

Negro slavery had been abolished in Mexico as early as 1829. African slaves were few in Mexico and were negligible from the economic point of view. Indeed, abolition had been intended to raise a barrier to a further influx of Americans and their slaves into northern Mexico, particularly Texas.

Jefferson Davis, Robert Toombs, Judah P. Benjamin —Confederate Secretary of State since March, 1862 [1]—and other ex-imperialists of the South, who in the years preceding the Civil War had been ardent advocates of United States expansion at the expense of Mexico, suddenly reversed their policies. They made secret offers of restitution of huge territories to the new Empire in return for recognition and a military alliance.

ONE OF THE MOST interesting documents revealing the state of mind of Davis and his associates in the critical months of 1863 was written by Edward T. Hardy, consular agent of the Austrian Empire in Norfolk, Virginia, and evidently also a Confederate agent in the Consular Service of Francis Joseph I. Entitled "The Aspect of American Affairs," Hardy's report was filed as an important document in the Imperial Chancery of Vienna.

Little is known of Hardy, except that he was Austrian Vice-Consul although an American citizen, and that he— with diplomatic caution—espoused the Confederate cause. Hardy claimed that he was not in direct contact with the Confederate government—otherwise he could not have stayed in Norfolk, a city occupied by Union troops—yet

[1] Toombs, who was too independent for Jefferson Davis, resigned as Secretary of State in July, 1861. His immediate successor was "yes-man" Robert M. T. Hunter, but he was soon replaced by Judah P. Benjamin.

he was extremely well informed about Southern intentions. The Austrian envoy in Washington and the Foreign Ministry in Vienna relied on his reports and connections, and he had been repeatedly asked to remain at his post, although he had expressed the desire to move, preferably to Canada. He left Norfolk and the Consular Service in January, 1865. Significantly, no successor to Hardy was appointed, although Norfolk's consular importance increased with the collapse of Southern resistance.

Hardy's sixteen-page handwritten report assumed that Archduke Ferdinand Maximilian's acceptance of the Mexican Crown was a foregone conclusion, and that, "an Empire having been proclaimed, a war with the United States is inevitable; and next in importance to the pacification and reconciliation of the people of Mexico is a recognition of the Southern Confederacy, and an alliance offensive and defensive with it." This sounds like an invitation to Maximilian from Jefferson Davis for a joint offensive against the Union.

Hardy expounds his view of world politics—and again it sounds as if President Davis or his Secretary of State Benjamin were speaking: "England will not lose the opportunity of weakening and humbling so gigantic a rival, neighbour, and moral antagonist. She has borne with subdued fury many insults during the last two years; but though the government has long been resolved on war, it is determined to provoke the declaration, not to make it. It cannot be long postponed. England and France will therefore probably be united with Mexico in the recognition of the Confederate states."

As the document expands in scope, it becomes more and more evident that it conveys the views of the Richmond government and is not just the private opinion of one of the most obscure Vice-Consuls in the Austrian Foreign Service. Indeed, it would have been regarded as an impertinence on the part of a minor employee—not even a baron or a chevalier—to annoy his superiors with such a long and presumptuous epistle, were it not assumed that he was acting as a relay for the Confederate government. Often enough foreign consular employees were used, and sometimes even arrested, as secret agents in the course of the Civil War.

This confidential but articulate voice of the Confederacy—coming from an American in the service of the Austrian Emperor—is worth printing in full:

The Aspect of American Affairs

As there must be some basis from which to start in the expression of opinion at such a period as now obtains, and as I am ignorant of the exact position of His Imperial Majesty, if indeed it be as yet definite, I have to assume a premise.

Nothing is more natural than that he should be, if not in "rapport," at least in sympathy with His brother the Archduke and elected Emperor of Mexico, and with all who are connected with the establishment of that Empire.

An Empire having been proclaimed, a war with the United States is inevitable; and next in importance to the pacification and reconciliation of the people of Mexico, is a recognition of the Southern Confederacy, and an alliance offensive and defensive with it.

The people of Mexico are said to be a good tempered race; easily led by a promise of good. Their discords have proceeded out of the conflicting designs of ambitious leaders. Persons that have traveled through the interior make frequent allusions to the simplicity of their natures. Inquiries concerning the institutions of this country are often noted, and one writer mentions particularly their expressed desire to have a free school system like that of some of the United States. The high castes, as is generally understood, are of Spanish descent, mostly of pure blood. The Mexicans make fair soldiers, and with good leaders and a thorough discipline, might be formed into very effective armies. They fought better against the French, than they did against the Americans. The cause may lie in the fact that the French were from another continent; or from the fear of being reduced to the condition of a province of the French Empire. The stability of the government proposed for them, seems to insure it a congenial reception on all sides.

The programme of the new Imperial Government might be, 1st The establishment of the Throne beyond peradventure: 2nd The recognition of the Southern States: 3rd If it be necessary, war in conjunction with the South and other allies against the Northern States: 4th If war, then the recovery of the State of California, and, if the Southern States will allow, of the *territory* of New Mexico; both of which were necessarily ceded to the United States under the treaty of Gaudaloupe Hidalgo.[2]

The State of Texas, which is a possible object with the Emperor of France, will be found impracticable. For 1st Its independence was acknowledged by Mexico before the war with the United States: 2nd It was an integral state of the Federal Union: 3rd It is now one of the Seceded States, all of which are pledged to the defence of its integrity: and 4th The people are of the most independant and jealous character, and would never consent.

The query occurs: If the Emperor of France after conquering Mexico and releasing it for ulterior designs, still purposes to retain for himself a foothold upon the continent, why is not the country to the South of Mexico suited to his views? It is as rich as Texas; is one of the most important on the continent as embracing the isthmus of Darien; and would be found much more controllable. A stable government would be as great a blessing to the people of that region as to Mexico: and now is a fit opportunity to propose it. Mexico should be an integrity from Oregon to Honduras.

France is necessarily involved in any present war between Mexico and the United States.

England will not lose the opportunity of weakening and humbling so gigantic a rival, neighbour, and moral antagonist. She has borne with subdued fury many insults during the last two years; but though the government has long been resolved

2 The Treaty of Guadaloupe Hidalgo, signed in 1848, ended the Mexican war and ceded most of the present Southwest of the United States.

on war, it is determined to provoke the declaration, not to make it. It cannot be long postponed. England and France will therefore probably be united with Mexico in the recognition of the Confederate States.

It is thought by many that Canada will not enter cheerfully upon a war with the United States. I know nothing of the present disposition of the Canadian population, except what is contained in the following extract from a letter written to me by a very intelligent and perfectly reliable man, who moved from here since the Federal occupation. He writes from Ottawa, the proposed capitol of Canada West, but has also resided in Port Hope and Toronto since leaving here. He says: "Here in Canada the English and Scotch part of the population and also the French are decidedly on the Southern side. If you could hear the conversation on the streets as news despatches are received and witness the manifestations of sympathy and good wishes for the Southern cause, you would imagine yourself in a Southern city." My belief is that this represents the sentiment of the entire people of Canada. In all the British Provinces the inhabitants entertain a repugnance towards Northerners.

Others are of the opinion that if Canada were erected into a separate kingdom under a British Prince, the people would be inspired with a more special loyalty, than is at present accorded to the distant government. It might not be inaffectual; but with good leaders the people would fight well under either government. Nor is there any encouragement in the aspect of republican institutions on this continent at present, to taint the Canadians with the idea of rebellion, and a consequent alliance with the North. I regard this as out of the question under its present liberal institutions.

This is a fearful aspect for the North, but will be met, not unwillingly, by men, who are seeking power, and profess that they cannot escape from history.

There is a new-sprung hope of an alliance with Russia. It will be pressed with vigor, but who can say with what success? Is Russia prepared to enter into an alliance offensive and defensive with a power having no interest in common with her, except that it is opposed to the Western Powers of Europe?—Whose institutions are the antipodes of those of Russia? —and every contact with which must leave contamination? As this is the most momentous question of the times, I trust to be pardoned for a few remarks.

I assume that the Polish question [3] is the only impediment to the impending action on this continent. It is not yet satisfactorily solved. And why not? It is plain to the outside world that the Czar has determined to extend the benign influence of liberal institutions to *all* his subjects, and will not be prevented by the present mistaken demonstrations in Poland. But the difficulty, which keeps apart an amiable Sovereign and a loyal people, has sprung from, and is sustained by, misapprehension. The Poles do not understand the kind feelings of their noble Monarch, and the Czar, though willing, is fearful of condescending too far. Prince Gorchakov has already, in his first reply, signified the intent of his august Master to extend to the Poles a government as liberal as they are prepared to receive, and in spirit progressive.

Knowing from his acts the magnanimity of the Czar, I have never believed that the Polish insurrection could result in anything serious. And when the Czar shall so far condescend as to make manifest by his words and his countenance, the benevolent intentions he entertains towards them, the Poles will lay down their arms and be happy to return to allegiance.

Since the first outbreak in Poland there has been a tenacious hope, that it would involve the Western Powers and inflame the republican sentiment all over Europe. The co-operation of all the restless elements was counted on: and then what a glorious opportunity to blot out forever the pretensions of England and France upon this continent. As the despatches of Earl Russell erected a firm attitude, the hearts of the Washington administration gloated with expectation. But now that it is too late to forbear the insults of Wilkes and others, or to retract the stand on the subject of vessels built in England for the South, their hopes will be much embarrassed, if not para-

[3] The Polish insurrection of 1863 against the Czar led to severe reprisals and Russification. It also strained relations between London-Paris-Vienna and St. Petersburg.

94

lyzed, by the recent developments in Polish affairs, to wit: the sending of General Prince Nicholas Mouravieff to pacify the Poles; and also an ambassador to Paris (late report), to offer a separate constitutional government for Poland.

It is not to be supposed that the Czar would form an alliance with the United States simply to make war upon the Western Powers; for he really designs to pacify the Poles, and then what further object could he have? Nothing—except the ambition, pure and simple, of being engaged in war; or the desire of conquest. In his short but glorious reign, he has manifested no symptom of either sentiment. If mere war was an object, could he not have protracted the Crimean war indefinitely? If conquest; was not that as fair an opening for an expectation, as is now afforded?

I would rather suppose, that the transparent character of Mr. Clay, the United States Minister at St. Petersburg, being recognized, he has been cajoled with the flattering hope of an alliance, to hasten, in harmony with the animus of the rest of Europe, the catastrophe, to which the United States is palpably tending. There may be discovered some plausible evasion, only after it is too late for the Washington Cabinet to recall their action.

Long negotiations seldom result in war; and the Western Powers, so soon as they shall have recognized a manifest intent on the part of the Czar to comply with the treaty of 1815, may avoid any further complications with him. Thus they will be free to meet the views of the Washington Cabinet, whose great purpose is *war*. War, not peace, is their programme. So it do not *exterminate* the people of the North, they do not care how much war they have. Why? Because war keeps them in Dictatorial power, at the head of immense armies. I may here remark that I can imagine no possible combination, that can defeat them in the next Presidential election.

The reclamation of the South into the Union is not so much an object, as to overrun the territory of the Southern States, and get soldiers to fight England, France, and Mexico. They do get negroes, who, though of a most peaceable nature, may be drilled into tolerable soldiers. It requires a little time to awaken their faculties to a battle. They are first employed in digging entrenchments, and are gradually led on to enlistment.

Their hope is further, to so far reduce the Southern States, as to inspire the people with despair of sustaining the government; and then to inflame them with an appeal to their traditional animosity against England, to their common cause in the enforcement of the Monroe doctrine, and also in the sentiment of republicanism. But white soldiers they will not get, even from those portions of the South that have long been in their possession. As for those within the Confederate lines, it is not to be thought of.

The enforcement of the recent conscription is a signal triumph of the administration. It is notorious that the riot in New York was constituted almost entirely of foreigners, principally Irish. Governor Seymour of New York is the only man that ever raised the expectation of opposition to the central power. Immediately after his inauguration, he showed that he lacked the spirit, and nothing further has been expected of him. Mr. Vallandigham, the only man that could raise an opposition, is banished. He may, or he may not be elected governor of Ohio. If he be, on the alarm of foreign war, he will side with the Administration. Although there is a strong and growing party in favour of peace, they do not, and for the present, will not, resist. The difficulty in the development of the Democratic party, (the opposition,) lies in the impracticability of the assertion of states rights, without falling under the imputation of *treason* to the Union, for the preservation of which the North purports to be fighting. In a foreign war the North will be united, and under good generals their soldiers are formidable.

The plan for procuring soldiers from the Southern people, is to exact of all that fall in their reach an oath of allegiance to the central power, to the exclusion of states rights. But though, by cruelty and threats, they have registered a great many oaths, they have enlisted but few men: and those who have taken the oath will disregard it, when there is encouragement of permanent reoccupation by the South. A few take it voluntarily to

Napoleon III, Emperor of France

His Empress, Eugénie

OPPOSITE: *President Lincoln's letter to Emperor Francis Joseph closing the so-called "Burlingame incident"*

Francis Joseph I, Emperor of Austria

The Archduke Maximilian, Emperor of Mexico

His Empress, Carlota

Abraham Lincoln,
President of the United States of America.

To His Imperial Royal Majesty,
Francis Joseph I,
Emperor of Austria
Great and Good Friend:
I have made choice of J. Lothrop
Motley, one of our most distinguished citizens, to reside near
Your Majesty in the quality of Envoy Extraordinary and Minister
Plenipotentiary of the United States of America. He is well
informed of the relative interests of the two countries, and of
our sincere desire to cultivate and strengthen the friendship and
good correspondence between us; and from a knowledge of
his fidelity, probity and good conduct, I have entire confidence
that he will render himself acceptable to Your Majesty by his
constant endeavors to preserve and advance the interests and
happiness of both nations. I therefore request Your Majesty to
receive him favorably, and to give full credence to whatever he
shall say on the part of the United States; and most of all when
he shall assure Your Majesty of their friendship and wishes
for Your prosperity. And I pray God to have Your Majesty
always in His safe and holy keeping.
Written at the City of Washington
this fifteenth day of August Anno Domini, one thousand
eight hundred and sixty one.
Your Good Friend,

Abraham Lincoln
By the President.

William H. Seward.
Secretary of State.

Abraham Lincoln

BELOW: *An article from the Richmond, Virginia, Sentinel which was forwarded by the Austrian Consul General in New York to the Austrian Chancellery in 1865. The article was believed to have been written by Jefferson Davis.*

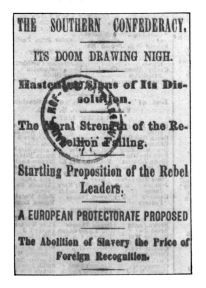

THE SOUTHERN CONFEDERACY,

ITS DOOM DRAWING NIGH.

Masterly Signs of Its Dissolution.

The Moral Strength of the Rebellion Falling.

Startling Proposition of the Rebel Leaders.

A EUROPEAN PROTECTORATE PROPOSED

The Abolition of Slavery the Price of Foreign Recognition.

RIGHT: *Newspaper clipping attached to the dispatch of Baron Wydenbruck to the Austrian court in which he reported the assassination of President Lincoln*

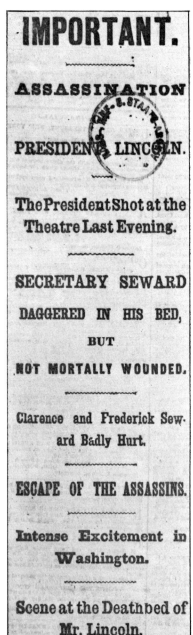

IMPORTANT.

ASSASSINATION

PRESIDENT LINCOLN.

The President Shot at the Theatre Last Evening.

SECRETARY SEWARD

DAGGERED IN HIS BED,

BUT

NOT MORTALLY WOUNDED.

Clarence and Frederick Seward Badly Hurt.

ESCAPE OF THE ASSASSINS.

Intense Excitement in Washington.

Scene at the Deathbed of Mr. Lincoln.

gain favor: others to attain places, of which they never before had a dream. Such are the present civil authorities of Norfolk.

The programme of the South is 1st Freedom: 2nd Under States rights, that is, the sovereignty of the individual state: 3rd Their territory; all the seceded States, including Tenessee, Missouri, and the Territory of New Mexico: 4th The offer to Kentucky and Maryland of their free choice to unite with South or North. It will be observed that I omit slavery, of which a few words presently.

The first and greatest states rights man in this country was Patrick Henry of Virginia. He was an extraordinary intuitive genius, who, reared a peasant, and without training, became the most distinguished orator amongst a galaxy of acknowledged great men. It was Henry, that precipitated the revolution, which led to a separation from Great Britain. He was the typical spirit, the representative man of the people, conscious by instinct of their rights, and jealous and restive of every and any encrochment upon them. With all his magnificent powers, for twenty days, he argued, wrestled, debated, protested, and besought, in the name of the people, against the combined talent of the land, for the perpetuation of the *Constitution of Confederation,* under the auspices of which the war of liberation had been carried on: and bitterly opposed the present constitution, which, he foresaw, tended to the establishment of a central power and to the evolution of sectional oppressions. His points were unanswerable, but his voice failed of its usual effect. His warnings were prophetic, and are now realized. It is a misfortune that the arguments and entreaties of this great man were never published among the other state papers, most of which are full of solicitude for the Union. He did not write his speeches, and his power over an audience is said to have been such, that no man could report them. Only a few fragments are preserved.

An essential argument on this subject, and one not usually marshalled to its defence, is in this wise: Montesquieu, in his "Spirit of Laws," asserts the principle that a republican form of government cannot be long sustained in any territory larger than a *city*. "Quoad hoc," the state of Virginia, or any individual state of the former Union, what with, 1st the modern advances in enlightenment; 2nd the progress in arts, whereby distance is neutralized and short separations disappear; 3rd the scanty population; and 4th their harmony of interest; might be regarded as representing the speculative embodiment of the "city" of Montesquieu. But, waiving nice points, the gist lies in that when a territory is so great as to cause antagonism of interest, or even of moral sentiments, there can be, under a republican government, no supreme head, *independent* of party or sectional prejudices and passions; who can afford to be as indifferent to the clamors of the strong, as sensitive to the cries of the weak; and able from extended experience to interpose with prudence and firmness between the fanatic and his victim, the plunderer and his quarry;—or to balance the justice of more equal antagonisms. An elected president must necessarily carry out the policy and designs of his party; 1st in gratitude for his election; 2nd to sustain the party and thereby his own authority; and 3rd to secure the next election. He cannot therefore be *impartial*. When the platform of the party is purely sectional, the election of its candidate is tantamount to a declaration of war. Such was the nature of Mr. Lincoln's election. How can an individual thus circumstanced prevent oppression to the section opposing him? Nay! instead of interposition for the weak, he is the exponent of their cruel foes. Hence the need, if the people are supposed to be Sovereign, of recognizing, in any Confederate association, that form of sovereignty, which approaches nearest to the people, and proceeds most immediately from them; and of providing such safeguards, that the smallest neighbourhood may enforce its own rights, or refuse its relations.

The greatest champion of the opposite sentiment, of consolidation, based on the sophistry that the authority delegated to the general government was a direct emanation from the people instead of the *States,* was the prodigious Webster, a man, to whose name every public man involuntarily gives place, but who gained a not less hollow and ephemeral triumph for his argument on this subject in reply to the elegant and brilliant address of Mr. Hayne of South Carolina, than he did for his answer to the dignified note of the Chevalier de Hülsemann remonstrating against the act of President Taylor in the establishment at Vienna of a "quasi" Hungarian Legation.

The people of the South have shown that they are in earnest. They hate their insane oppressors with an invincible malice. Nothing short of extermination will conquer them. Their unanimity has never been fully realized abroad, and has been constantly misrepresented in the Northern press. Since the proclamation of President Lincoln in April, 1861, the people have been literally an unit. There is some division only in sections bordering on the Northern States. The character of the people may be worth noting. As a mass, they are not so well educated as the people of the North, but are of a brighter nature and quicker instinct. They are not so shrewd in business but more honorable. This difference was notorious in reference to the members of congress from the opposite sections. From my little field of observation, I believe they are equal in tone and morality with the like number of any agricultural population in the world. Slavery has assuredly in that respect been no bane. It has been in other respects, and so has the policy of the South in several particulars, to which allusion need not now be made.

The South is willing to make concession in commercial negotiations, and in anything else that does not diminish her territory. This would as a rule apply to all republics, which with notions of freedom, would be reluctant to consign any of their population to opposing institutions. I know nothing of the animus of the government in this respect, but my own idea would be that if any could be spared, it would be New Mexico, an interior territory, thinly populated by emigrants and adventurers, and therefore in a more transferable form. It is thought to be as rich in minerals as any part of Mexico. I think the South would rather see California in possession of the Empire than of the Northern States. It would be a rich acquisition. It is not improbable that *definite* and *liberal* terms offered to the *Mormon population*, would secure their co-operation.[4] It would be a powerful aid in the rear of California. The Mormons are

[4] The idea of an alliance between the Catholic Empire of Mexico and the Mormons against Lincoln's Union, paradoxical as it sounds, was based on the existing hostility between the Mormons and Washington.

deeply exasperated against the United States, and when they emigrated to their present locality, did not dream that the United States would have so large a population to the West of them in so short a time. The population is estimated between seventy and eighty thousand, with a preponderance of females. The fighting element is probably as good as any in the country.

The subject of slavery is so difficult of representation to one who has not witnessed its operation in our Southern States, that it would be avoided if possible.

The Constitution of the United States solemnly sanctions and guarantees the institution, and recognizes slaves as property. It could not have been formed without such provisions.

The Southern people are of the same races as the Northern, and are fully their equals in humanity, morality and piety. Slavery was not of their seeking, but was forced on them, much against their will, by the government of Great Britain. Neither was it ever an object with the most intelligent of the population. They regard the negro as a great responsibility, forced on them thus perhaps for some wise purpose. The race has certainly been very instrumental in clearing malarious lands in the South, that would have been fatal to any white race. The leaders in the border states have been anxious for thirty years to initiate schemes for emancipation; but have been prevented by the sustained pressure of fanatical admonitions and threatenings from the North. The institution has therefore been a source of the keenest solicitude to our most sagacious statesmen, of whom Henry Clay was the fairest exponent. It has not been the bent and pride of the South, but her inevitable incubus.

Yet regarding affairs in their present attitude, reason as I may, I cannot escape the consciousness that, in the event of negotiations between the Powers of Europe and the Confederate States, if a pledge for gradual emancipation could be embodied, it would not only be a satisfaction to the people of Europe, high and low, but positive service to the South. It is a mistake to compare the Southern States with the West India islands in reference to emancipation. There, the abundance of indigenous productions enables the freed black to live without work. But he cannot subsist in any portion of the South without labour. If freed therefore he would naturally fall into the usual custom in agricultural districts, of hiring himself by the year or month. Their condition might be for a time worse than formerly, but would gradually assume a difficult character. Some by industry would attain property and comforts, whilst others would sink into idleness and squalor. Southern negroes are not irreclaimably indolent. The better people of the South, and such are the slave-holders, would easily reconcile themselves to the new state of things, and conform to circumstances with cheerfulness.

Though it was the immediate cause of the present war, the South is not fighting for the perpetuation of slavery. She only desired, in the Union or out of it, to be left alone to controul [sic] her own affairs: merely assuming that her people are as intelligent as those of the North, and are capable of making as wise a disposition of their institutions, as those who have nothing to do with them.

The war, so far as relates to the North itself, will terminate upon the doctrine of states rights, or end in a Sovereignty. Practically it is the latter now, but there is a powerful opposition, and though the Democratic party appear to be split, there is much ground to judge that they will eventually unite on the peace platform, and will be the cause of peace, if not the actual negotiators. When the people awake to a sense of their position, they will be extremely restive under a Dictator, and will struggle hard for a renewed constitution based on states rights.

Mr. Lincoln will probably be the re-elected next President. It is usual to regard him as inferior in intellect to some members of his cabinet, at the head of whom Mr. Seward is supposed to stand. But Mr. Lincoln wears well. As he is more honest, so he is more logical than the Secretary of State: as he is more original, so are his turns more unexpected: and notwithstanding his quaint manners and expressions, he is very shrewd and pointed in his observations and acts. I should regard him as a more formidable antagonist in any encounter than the Secretary, whose specious plausibilities are not always discreet.

The South is certainly much reduced and is taxed to her

utmost resources. The late reverses, some by bad management, others by supposed treachery, have had a very serious effect on the people at large, who cannot understand the position of affairs as the President and commanding Generals do. But though disheartened they still respond to the calls for men, and the elders are now filling the ranks that have been hallowed by the blood of their offspring. They will hail therefore with joy and gratitude the early announcement of a recognition from and an alliance with their neighbours and natural friends. If therefore it has been determined on, saving all prudent delay in view of preparations for inevitable hostilities, the sooner the fact is signified to them, (even though not otherwise published,) the better effect will it have on their affairs: not that they are likely to succumb, for they will not, but to cheer them and spare some suffering.

Respectfully submitted,

E. T. Hardy, V.C.

Vice Consulate of Austria

Norfolk, Va., 19th September 1863.

AS THE FORTUNES of the Confederacy declined, the suggestions, advices, and offers tendered unofficially by Vice-Consul Hardy were confirmed and repeated by Southern statesmen of official standing. Fifteen months after the date of Hardy's report, President Davis dispatched a Minister Plenipotentiary to Paris and London to offer the abolition of slavery and other concessions in return for French and British support. The special envoy, Duncan Farrar Kenner, arrived too late to perform any diplomatic function other than to gather condolences. And Jefferson Davis's last desperate effort to invoke the help of "European Protectors" was also a complete failure.

IX

DESPITE THE MILITARY RE-
verses of the Confederacy
and its rapidly deteriorating economic situation, the third
year of the Civil War saw the culmination of the imperial
efforts to reconquer North America.

Emperor Napoleon III, Emperor Francis Joseph I,
and Emperor Maximilian realized that they could no
longer count on a military victory of the South. Yet, they
hoped for—and were eager to contribute to—the prolonga-
tion of the Civil War, which would exhaust both partici-
pants, bring the South definitely within their orbit, and
reduce Northern resistance to their ambitions.

Mexico became the bridgehead and bastion of the imperial conquistadors, and France's Marshal Achille François Bazaine, with his excellently equipped army of approximately thirty thousand French soldiers, plus a few
thousand Mexican auxiliaries, defeated the stubbornly re-

sisting forces of Juárez. "The Indian," however, refused to give up; he fled to the north, and from his headquarters near the Rio Grande organized vigorous guerrilla warfare against the foreign invaders.

Nevertheless, the royalists of Mexico felt secure enough to establish their Empire and on June 12, 1864, they installed Maximilian and Charlotte in the capital's vermin-ridden "Imperial Palace," the neglected residence of the former Spanish Viceroys. The Emperor and the Empress of Mexico spent the first night in their dilapidated though beflagged palace on two disinfected tables transformed into temporary beds. From this festive day on, Their Majesties chose to be known as Emperor Maximilian (Maximiliano) and Empress Carlota, although to the bitter end Secretary of State Seward stuck to "Archduke Maximilian," or a "Habsburg Prince," and "Archduchess Charlotte."

In their efforts to please their Spanish-Mexican subjects, Emperor Maximilian and Empress Carlota, who had no children of their own, adopted a grandson of Don Agustín Iturbide, hero of 1821, to rear as their heir. Don Agustín Iturbide had proclaimed Mexican independence from Spain on February 24, 1821, and had crowned himself Emperor in May, 1822. However, after a brief rule he had to flee to Europe in 1823, and in an attempt to reclaim his throne he was executed. His grandson's mother, Alice Iturbide, was a United States citizen and asked Washington's intervention to regain custody of her son, three-year-old Agustín. Seward intervened through his Paris Ambassador but events made his efforts superfluous.

The young sovereigns soon moved into a new home, the incomparably beautiful castle of Chapultepec, not far from the capital and yet surrounded by a strange mixture of primeval forest and landscaped parks. Built by the Spanish Viceroys, partly as a summer residence and partly as a fortified castle dominating the Valley of Volcanoes,

Chapultepec was the worthy successor to the fabled golden palace of Montezuma which had once stood on these fantastic lava-basalt rocks.

Here they established their luxurious court and began to construct their dream-empire. Maximilian probably had the best of intentions to build his realm for the benefit of his subjects—but he was not satisfied with Mexico alone. Back in Vienna, he had tried to persuade his younger brother, Archduke Ludwig Victor, to accompany him to America and to marry one of the two daughters of Dom Pedro, Emperor of Brazil. Although he introduced many reforms and gained a measure of popularity, Dom Pedro was a holdover from America's monarchic past and of course sympathized with Maximilian and with the Napoleonic-Habsburg schemes to reintroduce the "monarchist principle" in republican America. Since he had no male heir, he was inclined to give his blessing to Maximilian's dynastic plan, which would have brought him a Habsburg son-in-law and the support of three emperors.

Maximilian had won the approval of Francis Joseph and his Foreign Minister Count Rechberg. In the traditional spirit of the Habsburgs, he wanted to acquire new lands for his House by a dynastic marriage. *"Tu Felix Austria Nube,"* well-known Latin maxim of the Habsburgs, meant, "You lucky Austria, marry [to acquire new territories]." His grand idea was to set up his younger brother as a sort of junior emperor in Brazil and then annex all small countries between Mexico and Brazil to his own Empire. The gigantic double Empire of the House of Habsburg in America would thus dominate the Western Hemisphere, and could intervene in the Civil War and triumph over its "bitter enemy" the United States, which, in Maximilian's words, "can scarcely await its internal consolidation in order to smash the throne to be erected in front of its gates." [1]

[1] Maximilian to Napoleon III, August 10, 1863.

But Maximilian's ardor was not shared by Archduke Ludwig Victor, ten years his junior and the playboy of the family. Ludwig Victor had neither the pompous self-righteousness of Francis Joseph nor the quixotic qualities of Maximilian; he admittedly preferred Vienna's wine, women, and waltz to crown and glory in the New World.

Ludwig was "frivolous," Maximilian complained in a letter to Emperor Francis Joseph of October 27, 1863:

With Your Majesty's permission, I went on Saturday, the 17th of this month, to Ischl and stayed there during the afternoon of the 18th and the 19th. I had an extensive and long talk with my parents (and also with Uncle Ludwig) about the Mexican affair and let them read some of the more important documents in order to explain the *true* situation to them since I found that they were on many points wholly misled by public opinion and the European press. I may flatter myself with having rectified most of the preconceived views, allayed the fears and, in particular, proved that the entire question was from the very beginning handled with calm and persistency; that not for a moment have I changed my principles; that the previously established plan was adhered to; and, above all, that dignity was observed all the time. My frank and honest talk was reciprocated with warm cordiality. Similar was my success—only with less effort—with Empress Caroline in Salzburg.

I informed Rechberg that I was to meet Ludwig during my excursion and asked him whether I should resume the talk on the Brazilian project, which he [Rechberg] had so wholeheartedly supported. I received a most affirmative answer by telegram. My conversation with Ludwig showed me that he is still far from pleased with the idea, yet, as it appeared to me, chiefly on frivolous grounds; he is unable to think of a life beyond the seas, he is afraid he would suffer from homesickness, and so on. Nevertheless, I have made some progress: he promised [Maximilian crossed out "promised" and inserted: "told"] me he would obey a formal command from Your Majesty; even though, as he expressed himself, only "as a martyr." Considering Ludwig's character, such a command would be most appropriate; it is not likely that he should, on his own initiative, tear himself away from his Viennese surroundings, so harmful to him; a mighty impetus is needed, an authority such as wielded by Your Majesty alone, to compel him to make a resolution—the advantages of which he realizes instinctively, but he lacks the strength required to make up his mind. I know the Emperor of Brazil, and I believe him to be the person who, by his energy tempered by reason, is able to guide Ludwig into a respectable, useful and active way of life— which, of course, he would consider his duty, if he were to guide his own son-in-law.

Your Majesty, in your wisdom, will do what you will deem best for Ludwig and most beneficial for the family.

I have also given a hint to Count Rechberg as to the result of my conversation.

Dynastic discipline was rigid, as witness the fact that Maximilian had asked the Emperor's permission to talk to his parents about Mexico and had obtained the Foreign Minister's approval of his plans regarding Brazil. And even though Maximilian asked for the Emperor's command, Ludwig Victor, probably because of the intercession of their mother, was permitted to remain an uncrowned Don Juan instead of becoming a martyred Don Quixote.

ALL THIS TOOK PLACE before Maximilian had accepted the "Crown of Montezuma" and set out on the Austrian frigate *Novara* to reclaim the American Empire of Charles V. But even after accession to his shaky throne, Maximilian refused to abandon his grandiose plan and placed great hope on Dom Pedro's cooperation. At the very beginning of his reign Maximilian sent his friend Count Ollivier de Resseguier, a former Austrian naval officer who had accompanied the Emperor to Mexico, on a secret mission to the small Central American republics. With the help of French diplomatic agents and the *ancien régime* of these countries Count Resseguier attempted to create a Latin American royalist conspiracy against the republican governments, with the ultimate aim of "joining the Mexican Empire" in a powerful union extending from the Rio Grande "to the Isthmus of Panama." [2]

The French agents were instructed to co-operate closely with Maximilian's emissaries in order to turn Guatemala, Honduras, El Salvador, Nicaragua, Costa Rica, and Panama into as many small Mexicos, where the large landowners and the clergy would invite the protection of the Mexican Empire. Naturally, agents of the United States supported the republican parties and governments of all these countries, and it soon became evident that the fate of all the Americas was to be decided by the rise or fall of the great Republic to the north.

MAXIMILIAN'S ORIGINAL attitude toward the Union and the Confederacy was predetermined by his political interests and influenced by the views of Napoleon and Eugénie. The resulting fictitious picture of America was further distorted in his mind by the biased reports of Imperial France's diplomatic representatives abroad, which were usually slanted and prejudiced.

Napoleon's Ambassador in Washington, M. Mercier, had from the very beginning of the Civil War urged recognition of the South, even at the risk of an armed conflict with the Union. His Excellency's colleague, Count Saligny, France's Ambassador to Mexico, went even further and demanded military intervention against the Republic of Mexico, pointing to the unique chance given by the Civil War to the imperialist powers of Europe. Both diplomats were friends of the Duke of Morny, and Saligny especially seemed to be involved in the Duke's financial speculations. The diplomatic reports coming from England were presented to the Paris court and to Maximilian by French Ambassador Count Flahaut de la Billarderie,

[2] French Consul General in Guatemala, Tallien de Cabarrus, to Count Ollivier de Resseguier, November 13, 1864.

natural father of the Duke of Morny, whose opinion, of course, happened to reflect the views of his powerful son.

Maximilian's primary source of information was complemented directly and indirectly by Mexican monarchist leader Hidalgo and Southern Commissioner Slidell, both members of the Morny clique. King Leopold contributed his own "American expert," the Belgian diplomat F. Kint de Roodenbeck, who was sent on a special mission to Francis Joseph and Maximilian. He submitted that the august dynasties of Europe could be saved from the destructive influence of America only by the establishment of the Mexican monarchy. Otherwise, he argued, "America, in collaboration with Europe's revolutionaries, might undermine the very basis of the traditional social order of Europe." [3]

VOICES OF WARNING could not shake Maximilian's confidence in his diplomatic advisers, who were backed by Napoleon, Eugénie, and his royal father-in-law, the old fox of Belgium. Also, he was only too willing to be misled by the few but vocal Mexican émigrés, who claimed that the majority of the people in their homeland would welcome Maximilian as their imported Emperor.

Some of the warnings never reached Maximilian; those which did were cast aside. Among the latter was a letter from United States Consul Richard Hildreth in Trieste—written possibly with the knowledge of the State Department—cautioning Maximilian and Charlotte against trying to challenge the violently antimonarchist people of Mexico and the hostility of the United States. Consul Hildreth implored the adventurous young couple not to endanger their lives "in a venture that is bound to end in disaster." Hildreth's letter arrived at Miramar in October,

[3] Kint de Roodenbeck to Maximilian, December 30, 1863.

1863, about two months before Maximilian was formally offered the "Crown of Montezuma" by a delegation of Mexican nobles and clerics. But there was no need to heed warnings when, at approximately the same time, King Leopold reassured his children of England's forthcoming support. The King noted that the British government refused to give formal assurances for fear of provoking the United States. But, he added, "eventually, England will surely be involved in war with them and therefore the establishment of the Mexican Empire is of great importance to them." [4]

Thus, Maximilian looked upon the Confederacy as his predestined ally, whereas the Union was the natural enemy of his imperial venture. Nevertheless, after the military reverses of the South in the second half of 1863, he grew more cautious and closely followed Napoleon's diplomatic tactics. Before leaving for Mexico, Maximilian appointed Hidalgo his Ambassador at the court of Napoleon III. On this occasion he instructed his new envoy to "maintain strictly official relations with the Ambassador of the United States, and unofficial but warm personal relations with the Commissioner of the Confederacy."

JEFFERSON DAVIS, former champion of United States expansion at the expense of Mexico, welcomed the new Emperor by appointing an envoy extraordinary and minister plenipotentiary to "His Imperial Majesty, Maximilian." However, the eminent Southern gentleman, William Preston, failed to bring about a defensive and offensive alliance between the two neighboring countries as had been expected by the Davis government. The declining fortunes of the Confederacy made Maximilian wary of any provocation of Washington, and he tried hard to establish official relations with the Union

[4] Charlotte's Memo of her "Conversations avec cher Papa," October 12–19, 1863.

government. But as far as Lincoln was concerned, Maximilian did not exist. The United States envoy remained accredited to President Juárez, although "The Indian" was driven from his capital and his government was scarcely more than a myth.

Lincoln and Seward steadfastly rejected all attempts at *rapprochement* on the part of the Emperor. His envoys were not received, his personal emissaries and mediators were told that the United States recognized only the Juárez government, and his letters remained unanswered. Seward had warned the European powers against the Mexican adventure before Maximilian's arrival in the New World. Afterward, no opportunity was lost to show that the United States government regarded Maximilian as a foreign usurper and his Empire as a violation of the Monroe Doctrine. Nevertheless, Lincoln stuck to his principle of "one war at a time," and open conflict with France, the real power in Mexico, was scrupulously avoided.

DURING THE FIRST MONTHS of his rule, Emperor Maximilian continued to pursue his imperialist aims. He did not have much difficulty in obtaining recognition from most European countries. Even overcautious England ordered her navy to accord imperial honors to his flagship, the *Novara*, on its way to Mexico. And after some delay Her Britannic Majesty appointed an Ambassador to Imperial Mexico. Yet, Conquistador Maximilian had to face certain inconvenient facts, among others that the bulk of his army was under the command of French Marshal Achille Bazaine, who was responsible to Napoleon. To reduce his military dependence, Maximilian tried to raise a native army. This, however, increased his financial dependence since he was forced to borrow greater sums from the French treasury. Trying to raise "native" money, he increased his political dependence on the Mexican aristocracy and clergy, who demanded that he revoke all liberal legislation, including the land reform of the previous regime. Attempting to appease the now ruling class with half-measures, Maximilian increased popular antagonism against his own government while failing to satisfy the large landowners and the Church of his adopted country.

But Maximilian still had the seemingly boundless confidence and support of Napoleon, who found his half-measures agreeable, although Empress Eugénie was of a different opinion. "The proverbial wisdom of wielding an iron hand in a velvet glove was never so valid as in the case of Latin peoples—particularly those of Mexico," she wrote to Empress Carlota on July 30, 1864.

The young imperial couple was also encouraged by military reinforcements from Europe: in the winter of 1864-65, six thousand Austrian volunteers arrived, under the command of General Count Francis Thun-Hohenstein, and Belgium sent twelve hundred men, led by Lieutenant Colonel Van Der Smissen.

Maximilian's self-assurance rose when he set himself the task of organizing a tripartite army. The French forces remained under the command of Marshal Bazaine, the Austro-Belgian Brigade of Volunteers under Count Thun-Hohenstein, and his Mexican Imperial Army under General Mejia. The Emperor was not yet aware of the rivalries and jealousies inherent in such an incongruous army. He hoped for more volunteers from both sides of the Atlantic and saw himself as a crusader for monarchy and an enlightened *ancien régime* in the New World.

If Maximilian had known the Austrian Emperor's secret instructions to Count Thun, he would have been considerably less confident of becoming the arbiter of the Western Hemisphere.

Francis Joseph, in effect, saved his face but forsook his brother.

X DURING THE CRUCIAL PERIOD
between late spring of 1863
and early 1865, Emperor Francis Joseph had three different envoys accredited to Lincoln's government. After
twenty-five years of faithful service in the "unhealthy, un-
finished, and crude" capital of the United States, lacking
comfort though not excitement, Chevalier Huelsemann
asked to be retired. He left America on a leave of absence
on June 4, 1863—just one month before Gettysburg and
Vicksburg, and barely missing the triumphal entry of Napoleon's army in Mexico City.

Huelsemann's successor was Count Nicholas de Giorgi,
scion of a Dalmatian aristocratic family, who lasted until
November 8, 1864, when he suddenly died of a kidney
disease. The third Minister Plenipotentiary of His Austrian
Majesty was Baron Carl von Wydenbruck, who, like his
predecessors, sympathized with the South but saw more

clearly than any of them the approaching victory of the North.

Both Count Giorgi and Baron Wydenbruck received instructions from Vienna similar to those given to Count Thun-Hohenstein, commander of the Austrian volunteers sent to Mexico. The gist of the instructions was that His Majesty's government was "firmly resolved to maintain strict neutrality in the war between North and South and will keep hands off future developments in Mexico," stressing the fact that Mexico was a "purely private affair" of Emperor Maximilian.[1]

The League of the Three Emperors had begun to crack under the impact of Francis Joseph's imperial wrath.

THE PERSONAL RIVALRY of Francis Joseph and Maximilian had assumed the proportions of a dynastic feud by the time Maximilian set sail for Mexico. In the course of the negotiations between the two brothers, Francis Joseph—after graciously granting a loan and permission to recruit volunteers for the Mexican Empire—suddenly raised an unexpected condition. He demanded that Maximilian renounce his rights of succession to the Austrian throne.

Maximilian was second in line; first in line was little Crown Prince Rudolf, son of the Austrian Emperor. Maximilian protested and refused to sign the "family pact." But Francis Joseph was adamant; he made all his previous promises and his support of the Mexican enterprise contingent on the acceptance of his demand. Maximilian accused his older brother of "robbing him of his birthright." The Emperor made it clear that he did not expect Maximilian ever to return to Austria. Finally, Maximilian gave in and signed on the dotted line.

But during the long sea voyage on the *Novara*, Maxi-

[1] Instructions to Count Giorgi, February 1, 1864, to Count Thun, October 16, 1864, and to Baron Wydenbruck, February 1, 1865.

milian's resentment was fanned by the storms of the Atlantic and by his proud wife. In a very undiplomatic note he called the attention of the ruling houses of Europe—he and Charlotte were related to nearly all of them—to the "injustice" and questioned the validity of his renunciation "under pressure."

This was an unpardonable act of mutiny in the eyes of Francis Joseph, who insisted on the righteousness of his attitude as head of the House of Habsburg. He claimed that by becoming the sovereign of a foreign state, Maximilian had forfeited his right to succession in the old Habsburg Empire. And should Maximilian ever be forced to abdicate, it would be inadmissible to place a bankrupt ruler on the imperial throne of Austria.

IN ONE OF THE EARLY secret instructions sent by Austrian Foreign Minister Count Rechberg to Count Giorgi, on May 23, 1863, the imperial envoy was told "not to let President Lincoln be unaware of the substance of your instructions," namely, that Austria adhered to a "line of perfect neutrality" between North and South. As to the arrival of the six thousand Austrian volunteers in Mexico, the President and his Secretary of State were persuaded that it was a face-saving gesture and that Maximilian could expect no major military help from the Emperor of Austria.

There was, of course, much excitement in the Union on establishment of the Mexican Empire. In April, 1864, Congress denounced the erection of a "monarchical government" in America "under the auspices of any European power." There was a popular outcry at numerous demonstrations against the three Emperors and their invasion of Mexico. But, true to Lincoln's maxim, "one war at a time," an armed conflict was avoided, and his diplomatic moves were aimed at the division of the three associated powers. Strong United States protest notes were addressed to Napoleonic France, whereas Francis Joseph's Austria was treated with courtesy and Maximilian's Empire was ignored.

The rapid gains of the Union and the corresponding decline of the Confederacy induced Napoleon to appease Washington at the expense of Richmond. When United States Ambassador Dayton, armed with captured documents, protested against the construction of two ironclads and four corvettes for the Confederacy in French shipyards, Napoleon promised speedy redress. Countermanding his own orders—which, of course, he never admitted—the Emperor gave urgent instructions to cancel the "illegal" contracts. The six vessels, the future pride of the Confederate Navy, were lost before they were launched; they were sold to Prussia, Denmark, and Peru without consultation with the Commissioners of the South.

Napoleon had also grown keenly observant of international laws. When the famous Confederate raider, the British-built *Alabama* (which had captured and sunk about seventy United States merchant ships), sought refuge in the French port of Cherbourg, she was forced to leave, although outside the harbor the Union's powerful cruiser, the *Kearsarge*, was lying in wait. On June 19, 1864, after a spectacular but unequal fight, the *Alabama* was sent to the bottom.

NAPOLEON WAS ACCUSED of "deception" and a "violation of faith" by spokesmen of the South.[2] Southern sentiment turned against France, and Seward saw a chance to revive his old theory that a common enemy might reunite Americans on both sides of the battle line. The two most influential editors of the time, James Gordon Bennett of the New York *Herald* and Hor-

[2] Bulloch to Stephen R. Mallory, Confederate Secretary of the Navy, and Mallory's reply. Official records of the Union and Confederate Navies.

ace Greeley of the New York *Tribune*, were champion-
ing the idea of peace negotiations. Lincoln was skeptical
but gave his approval to an unofficial try.

The most interesting of several unofficial peace missions was that of Francis P. Blair, Sr., father of Montgomery Blair, Lincoln's controversial Postmaster General.
Lincoln's old friend went to Richmond and told Davis that
an honorable truce might be obtained if Davis would join
the North in sending armed forces against the French
army in Mexico to drive out both the French and Maximilian. Davis agreed to send a commission "to enter into
conference to secure peace to the two countries." Lincoln
replied that he was, as usual, "ready to receive any agent
. . . with the view of securing peace to the people of our
one common country." And so Lincoln emphasized his
one condition for peace—at the end of hostilities the Confederacy was to submit to national authority under the
Constitution.

Lincoln and Seward met with three Southern Commissioners, led by Confederate Vice-President Alexander
Stephens, on the Union ship *River Queen* at Hampton
Roads on February 3, 1865. Lincoln explained that "the
restoration of the Union is a *sine qua non* with me." [3]
When Stephens broached the "continental question" on
which they could get together, Lincoln said that Blair had
spoken in Richmond on Mexican matters without his au-
thorization. The conference ended without result.

THE PEACE-THROUGH-WAR idea,
involving war against Mexico and France, was never taken
seriously by Lincoln. Nor was he willing to initiate new
bloodshed. Lincoln's feelings in this respect coincided with
those prevalent in high diplomatic circles. Presumably re-
flecting the views of Lord Palmerston, his friend, Count
Rudolf Apponyi, Austrian Ambassador in England, re-

[3] Alexander H. Stephens, *Constitutional View, Recollections.*

ported to Vienna on April 25, 1863, on the altercation between Washington and London regarding the blockade of Confederate ports: "The fear that a war with England would reunite the North and the South . . . seems puerile to me, because the first act of hostility on England's part would be the recognition of the South which certainly would not reject the hand that can assure its independence." The South's position vis-à-vis France was essentially the same as that toward England.

Count Apponyi's report contains some further highly interesting observations: "A war with America would be infinitely more popular here than a war against Russia in favor of Poland. [Political intervention in favor of the Polish revolution against Russia created new tensions between the British and the Russian Empires.] England does not make war for an idea. The Polish cause is for her a matter of sentiment and by no means a matter of interest. But it is not the same with America since in this matter England has its honor to uphold, has affronts to avenge, and its most vital commercial interests to safeguard."

The Count then glanced over the English Channel and opined: "France would probably join England in this latest action [against the United States] because, in addition to the ill-will manifested by the Cabinet of Washington in regard to the Mexican expedition . . . Emperor Napoleon will perhaps not be too unhappy to see England engaged in a distant war, which might give him ample elbow room for his eventual designs."

MAXIMILIAN WAS PERHAPS the last to realize that he was virtually abandoned by his brother, for despite their feud he trusted the word of the Emperor and counted on the assistance of the Habsburg Empire. He also failed to realize the danger of Napoleon's change of policy toward the Confederacy and blindly relied on the "irrevocable" promises of the French Emperor. In Washington and in London he was soon dubbed "Archdupe Maximilian."

At the beginning of his reign, Maximilian invited his bitter adversary Juárez to meet him to explore the possibility of co-operation for the benefit of a new Mexico. Probably the young Emperor also believed that an external "cause"—his planned aggrandizement of Mexico—would bring about an internal unity of his adopted nation. This move, although a total failure, was symbolic of the good will and the liberal ideas of Maximilian, who in his old country had often shown his sympathy for the rebels against his older brother's authoritarian regime.

Indeed, the Emperor, who received his crown from the hands of a counterrevolutionary and ultraconservative minority of Mexico, tried sincerely to win over the republican revolutionaries by indicating his desire to create a liberal constitutional monarchy. But when suspicion on both sides foiled his plans, and intrigues among his French, Austrian, and native supporters increased his feeling of insecurity, he gradually abandoned his old ideas and sought escape in tyranny. This not unusual development culminated in his decree of October 3, 1865, outlawing Juárez and his followers, and authorizing the summary execution of all captured "enemies of the Empire."

MAXIMILIAN'S DREAM of a mighty double Empire to dominate the New World vanished as soon as the weakness of his rule in Mexico became apparent. But he still trusted his "destiny" and was, anyway, too proud to think of abdication. There was no lack of advisers and advice, each contradicting the other. Empress Eugénie urged Maximilian to concentrate on Mexico and forge its unity with "an iron hand"; Jefferson Davis desperately tried to draw Maximilian and Napoleon into war with the Union; some of his Mexican faithful sought to persuade him to get rid of his "foreigners" and rely on a purely Spanish-Mexican army and administration. The most original advice was perhaps that of Austrian Ambassador in Washington Count Giorgi, who proposed the formation of a "customs union" between the United States and the Mexican Empire.[4] Less original but more realistic was Secretary of State Seward, who said repeatedly and with increasing clarity that the Austrian Prince should get out of Mexico.

ABRAHAM LINCOLN's re-election on November 8, 1864, was not a sweeping victory; he received 55.09 per cent of all votes cast against 44.91 per cent for McClellan, although in the Electoral College vote Lincoln had a majority of 212 to General McClellan's 21. Even so, his re-election probably impressed all three Emperors. The famous words of his second inaugural, "With malice toward none; with charity for all . . . let us strive on to finish the work we are in . . . and cherish a just, and a lasting peace, among ourselves, and with all nations," may have reassured them to some extent. But most impressive, no doubt, was the report that by March, 1865, almost a million men were on Lincoln's muster rolls.

Baron Wydenbruck wrote to his new chief, Austrian Foreign Minister Count Mensdorff-Pouilly, on March 31, 1865: "The immeasurable resources raised by the American people made them eminently conscious of their power and of the role they are entitled to play in world affairs. The maritime powers of Europe will be obliged more than ever to pay attention to this proud and sensitive people."

[4] Giorgi to Rechberg, December 21, 1863.

XI

IN THE EARLY PART OF 1865, the military situation of the Confederacy was desperate and its economic condition hopeless. Its treasury was close to bankruptcy and its credit was wiped out by inflation. The Union armies under General Grant and General Sherman were constantly increasing their pressure on the exhausted forces of General Lee and General Johnston, who were suffering from lack of equipment, defeatism, and wholesale desertions.

President Davis, however, believed in miracles, and in himself, strongly enough to oppose serious peace negotiations, even when popular demand forced him to agree to Vice-President Stephens's exploratory talks with Abraham Lincoln. Davis's instructions were calculatedly unacceptable: he demanded from the near-victorious North the recognition of the Confederacy—the very thing Lincoln had been fighting against for nearly four years.

Davis fanatically rejected all counsel in favor of a compromise and steadfastly demanded the continuation of the hopeless struggle.

Undoubtedly West Pointer Davis, who prided himself on his military acumen, was fully aware of the desperate plight of his diminishing army. Also, he must have known better than any other member of his Cabinet the financial predicament of his Confederacy, deprived of its gold, its harbors, and its markets. He saw its cotton go up in flames, and witnessed at first hand the paralyzing effect of the "iron famine" on its defenses.

What, then, was the reason for Davis's apparently foolhardy "no compromise, no surrender" attitude? Was his boldness stimulated by promises of his former unofficial allies abroad? Did he expect last-minute help? Was he in possession of some grandiose plan of salvation? In his own memoirs, *The Rise and Fall of the Confederate Government*, Davis gives no acceptable explanation. But a diplomatic report in the former Imperial Archives of Vienna yields a clue to these one-hundred-year-old questions.

THE REPORT WAS SENT to Foreign Minister Count Mensdorff-Pouilly on January 6, 1865, by Chevalier Carl F. von Loosey, Austrian Consul General in New York. Loosey was in charge of all consular agents in the United States (North and South), including Vice-Consul Hardy. Loosey also sympathized with the South and he was in constant touch with Maximilian of Mexico.

During the interval between Count Giorgi's death and Baron Wydenbruck's arrival, Consul General Loosey was Chargé d'Affaires of the Austrian Legation, sending regular diplomatic communications to Vienna. In his dispatch of January 6th, he calls the attention of the Foreign Minister to an article of unusual importance in the Richmond *Sentinel*.

"Persons familiar with the style of expression of President Davis," asserted Loosey, "claim that this article was written by him. Secretary of State Seward attributes highest significance to the article, which faithfully reflects the situation in the South and the intentions of Jefferson Davis, according to a Washington source. Mr. Seward gave instructions to United States representatives abroad to make use of the article in order to prove that the rebel government's head himself admitted the failure of their enterprise: his government is exhausted, it is seeking help abroad and therefore it can no longer be recognized as a belligerent power. . . . "

Loosey attached to his report President Davis's *ballon d'essai*, which was widely discussed both in the South and in the North. The Richmond *Sentinel's* article said in part:

It becomes us coolly and calmly to look into the circumstances of our conditions. . . . It is childish to whine under misfortune. . . . It is cowardly to sink under it. . . .

We think that our reverses have done much toward preparing the minds of our people for the most extreme sacrifices if they shall be adjudged necessary. . . . [Our government] must take care, whatever befall us, to save us from the Yankees. If adverse gales and devouring billows should constrain our storm-lost ship into some port, let it be no Yankee port. Of all the people on earth, we should have most reason to loath and to dread them. Any terms with any other would be preferable to subjugation to them.

We lately published . . . a suggestion that, in the event of being unable to sustain our independence, we should surrender it into the hands of those from whom we wrested or purchased it, into the hands of Britain, France and Spain, rather than yield it to the Yankees.

From the favor with which this suggestion has been received, we are sure that in the dread event which it contemplates, our people would infinitely prefer an alliance with European nations on terms as favorable as they could desire, in preference to the dominion of the Yankees.

We speak of them not out of gloomy forebodings, but simply as a man in health speaks of his will.

WAS THAT MAN making his testament Jefferson Davis? Secretary Seward and Consul General Loosey thought so. The latter pointed to a simultaneous article in the Richmond *Enquirer* (both were published January 2, 1865) which said among other things:

> If it be necessary to convince the world that we are fighting for the self-government of the whites, that we should liberate the negroes, and if that liberation can be made to secure our recognition and the guaranty of England and France to our independence, we believe that the people of these states would not hesitate to make the sacrifice.
>
> In such light only do we understand the declaration of the Richmond *Sentinel.*

Had Jefferson Davis received any encouragement from the European powers? It is difficult to believe that anyone in a responsible position would have made an official statement to that effect in the last days of the Civil War. But unofficial advice and nonbinding promises are a different matter.

IN HIS SAME REPORT dated January 6th, Loosey underlined certain rumors "circulating in Washington" of a new form of recognition under consideration by England and France. "These two powers might declare after March 4th, the second inauguration of the President," Loosey said, "to recognize Lincoln as President of only those States of the Union which were represented in the electoral college. This would be equivalent to the recognition of the Confederate States."

Fantastic as it sounds, Consul General Loosey's report had a solid basis—at least so far as Jefferson Davis was concerned. Around the time of the Hampton Roads "peace conference," Davis had dispatched his Special Envoy Duncan Farrar Kenner to Paris and London, for the very purpose of offering the abolition of slavery in return for French and British support. Since it was a desperate, last-minute move, it is likely that Davis proposed the creation of a European "protectorate" out of the remnants of the Confederacy. Davis seemingly believed in it, even though nobody else did. But it was too late for diplomatic negotiations. The end was rapidly approaching.

Davis vetoed peace proposals to the Union whenever he was able, and obstructed them when open opposition was not feasible. Maybe he sincerely "loathed and feared" the Yankees and believed that any peace would mean "subjugation" by them. Probably he was a fanatic in his opposition to reunion. But he certainly was not a madman, and he must have visualized an alternative to total destruction. This alternative was, according to Seward and Loosey, the idea of a European "protectorate" and this idea was possibly created in Davis's mind by previous lavish promises of European rulers and their ministers. Davis also saw the establishment of a European protectorate in neighboring Mexico by European armies, and he may have remembered the unofficial discussions about offering a "Southern Crown" to a European prince in exchange for recognition and support of the secession.

Was Davis, in his despair, willing to abdicate in favor of a European prince rather than to surrender to Lincoln? Understandably Davis, suspicious at the height of his power and distrusting everybody toward the end of it, would never have put his signature under such proposals. But if the unsigned article in the Richmond *Sentinel* was not written by him, it was in all probability authorized by him and reflected his thoughts.

HOWEVER, IT WAS too late. All the crowns, and all the slaves of the Americas, would not have induced the powers of Europe to take up arms against a victorious United States. The formerly belligerent envoys of England and France in Washington were replaced, and the Austrian Ambassador was the first to congratulate Secretary of State Seward on the fall of Richmond,[1] although it was evidently a heavy blow to Maximilian. Soon Wydenbruck suggested the elevation of the Austrian Legation in Washington to the rank of an Embassy.

Another sign of the European powers' increasing disregard for the South can be found in a short note of December 5, 1864, from the Austrian Ambassador in Paris, Prince Metternich, to his Foreign Minister accompanying a copy of the "Southern Manifesto." The usually voluble Prince forwarded the Manifesto, to which so much importance was attached by the people of the Confederacy, without a word of comment, indicating that it was not worth reading. Metternich only observed that the Manifesto was brought to him by "Mr. Erlanger, the son-in-law of Mr. Slidell, Commissioner of the Confederate States," and that "Mr. Slidell, having never entertained any official relations with the Imperial Government," chose this way of delivery "in order to maintain the semiofficial character of this *démarche* for the convenience of the imperial government."

Needless to say, this "backdoor" diplomatic status was not Mr. Slidell's choice.

The "Manifesto of the Congress of the Confederate States of America," while attempting to justify its "defensive" war, was essentially an attempt to invoke a new European peace mediation. An attached Joint Resolution requested President Davis to transmit the Manifesto to "our commissioners abroad" for the purpose of submitting it to "foreign Governments." The Manifesto was "approved June 14, 1864," but it was not until the following Decem-

[1] Wydenbruck to Mensdorff-Pouilly, April 4, 1865.

ber 5th that it was forwarded by Commissioners Slidell, Mason, and Mann. Was it the hand of Davis which delayed the diplomatic transmission of this document until the situation of the South had become critical?

THE PRESIDENT of the Confederacy was not "demented" as Vice-President Stephens had suspected after Davis's "fight till final victory" speech following the failure of the Hampton Roads peace conference.[2] But he obviously suffered from the delusion that a Northern victory would not be tolerated by the great powers of Europe. He would not accept the fact that he had been abandoned by Napoleon III and his puppet Emperor Maximilian, and that he was regarded as expendable by all European rulers.

Even after the fall of Richmond, on April 3, 1865, when Davis fled his capital to seek security with General Johnston's army, he declared at Johnston's headquarters that he intended to raise more soldiers and would "whip them yet."

Less than a week later, on April 9th, General Lee surrendered at Appomattox Courthouse after he had ignored Davis's frenzied demand to continue the hopeless fight. When General Johnston, too, told him that further resistance would be a crime, Davis refused to surrender with Johnston and escaped.

DAVIS HATED LINCOLN with a cold, irreconcilable fury, whereas Lincoln regarded him with a mixture of pity and contempt. He had no desire to capture and punish him. At a Cabinet meeting Lincoln spoke out against harsh treatment of the rebels, and said: "No one need expect me to take any part in hanging or killing these men, even the worst of them. Frighten them

[2] Alexander Hamilton Stephens, *Recollections*.

out of the country, open the gates, let down the bars, scare them off. . . .

"Shoo," Lincoln added, according to a Cabinet member witnessing the scene, and he threw up his hands like a man scaring sheep.[3] Less than another week passed and Lincoln died at a Southern assassin's hand.

[3] Gideon Welles, *Diary*.

XII

"Ma main tremble . . ."
"My hand is trembling as I write these lines." The opening words of Baron Wydenbruck's report on the assassination of President Lincoln are an eloquent tribute to the man who gained the respect and even the admiration of some of his greatest adversaries.

The envoy of Emperor Francis Joseph I happened to be in New York on the fatal night of April 14-15. He wrote his first dispatch in New York and returned immediately to Washington. In this hastily written account to His Excellency Count Mensdorff-Pouilly, the envoy gave a brief and fairly accurate description of the assassination:

> New York, April 15, 1865
> 6:30 in the morning
>
> My Lord,
> My hand is trembling as I write these lines. At the very moment when I was about to enter my carriage to catch a

train to Washington, I learned that President Lincoln was murdered last night about ten o'clock in his private box at the theater. The murderer, who had entered the box un-noticed, fired a pistol shot at the President's neck. The bullet traversed his brain and left through the forehead. At the moment I write, the news of his decease has not yet been re-ported. The suspected assassin is an actor of the name of Booth known to be a fanatical partisan of the South.

Before jumping from the box to the stage, the assassin, brandishing a dagger, cried out "Sic semper tyrannis" [Ever thus to tyrants], the motto of the state of Virginia. Then he crossed the stage and disappeared. A horse awaited him at the theater door, enabling him to escape.

At the very moment of this tragic scene, a series of murder attempts took place in the house of the Secretary of State. A stranger called on him, on the pretext of being sent by Mr. Seward's doctor. On his way to the Secretary's bed-room he encountered Undersecretary of State Frederick Seward, the State Secretary's son, who tried to prevent his entry. The stranger repeatedly stabbed Frederick Seward, who collapsed. Then the assassin entered the Secretary's room, attacked and wounded several persons he found there, and threw himself on Mr. Seward. The Secretary of State, bedrid-den because of a previous accident,[1] was stabbed several times in the throat and in the breast. None of his wounds is mortal, but it is to be feared that, in his already precarious state, the loss of blood might be fatal to him. The condition of his son, too, is alarming.

I request Your Excellency to excuse me kindly for the haste in which these lines have been written. I have not even had time to draw a copy since my trunk is about to be locked.

Please accept, my Lord, my deep respect.

Wydenbruck

(P.S.) The President has just died. I write to the Austrian Consul in Queenstown who will cable the news to Your Excellency in due course.

---

[1] Only a week before the assassination attempt, Secretary Seward had fallen from his carriage when his horses bolted, and had suffered multiple fractures.

In a later dispatch of April 18th to Count Mensdorff-Pouilly, Baron Wydenbruck reported the condolences of the diplomatic corps and then said: "The deep mourning in which the tragic end of the President has plunged the country . . . appears as unanimous as it is sincere. This proves more than all the panegyrics to what extent Mr. Lincoln had captured the affection, the respect, and the trust of the American people. Simple and modest in his tastes and his manners, just and honest in all ramifications of his private and political life, and with a great benevolence of character, Mr. Lincoln sinned only in one respect: that of yielding too easily to the pleading of those who surrounded him. . . . Be that as it may, from the moment when the reverses of the Confederacy and the dissolution of its government had opened the way to the re-establishment of the Union, Mr. Lincoln's spirit of moderation and conciliation has won the upper hand in all deliberations.

"From this point of view, the death of Mr. Lincoln is equally a misfortune for the South, for the South is accused of having thrust the weapon into the assassin's hand. It is almost certain that this murder was the result of a long-range conspiracy, which planned also the assassination of Vice-President Andrew Johnson and all the members of the Cabinet."

This was generally assumed at the time and, in particular, Jefferson Davis was suspected of being involved in the conspiracy. At the beginning of May, a government proclamation announced that the Bureau of Military Justice had evidence of the guilt of Davis and set a price of one hundred thousand dollars on his head.

BUT THEIR MAJESTIES in Paris and Mexico were of different opinions. In particular, Empress Eugénie defended the Southern gentlemen and tried to shift the blame to the Northern "radicals." She wrote to Empress Carlota on April 30th:

131

"The assassination of Lincoln has created a great sensation in Europe. Some accuse the South. To me, however, it seems more probable that the radicals in the North are responsible, those who considered the President too moderate."

Eugénie did not shed tears over the tragic death of her great adversary, although the assassination of the head of a state was, of course, repugnant to her on principle. Carlota's attitude was similar except that she seemed to be even less informed and more hopeful of profiting by the change of leadership in the United States. In a letter of April 27th to Eugénie she commented:

"The announcement has just been received by telegraph that President Lincoln, his son, and Mr. Seward have been assassinated [*sic*]. I think this will lead to Mac Clellan's [*sic*] becoming President and to some sort of settlement with the South."

LINCOLN'S SUCCESSOR, President Andrew Johnson, was almost entirely unknown abroad. Now he was suddenly thrust into the limelight of world politics. Baron Wydenbruck in his report of April 18th, commented:

"In his inaugural address he abstained from establishing a program of his future policy, leaving, he said, circumstances to take care of directing the path. However, in judging him by his past policy and previous statements, he might be expected to be less inclined than was his predecessor to a course of generosity and conciliation."

Ten days later, Wydenbruck found his estimate confirmed by events. He noted that the hiding place of John Wilkes Booth was discovered, and the assassin, who refused to surrender, was shot by Federal troops. He added: "President Johnson recently declared that the South as a whole was an accomplice in the murder of Mr. Lincoln.

Mr. Stanton, Secretary of War, outdid him by asserting that the plot had been contrived in Canada and approved by Richmond. In vain one asks what the purpose of such denunciations may be now that the Confederacy is about to expire and the time has come to calm the spirits and appease animosities. . . . "

He grew more critical when describing the events that followed the capitulation proposal of General Johnston, whose army of 30,000 faced that of General Sherman "counting no less than 120,000 men." Sherman offered very liberal conditions.

"General Sherman was subject to severe disapproval by a Cabinet council convoked by the President," Wydenbruck continued. "He was ordered to resume hostilities without delay and to accept no surrender of the Confederate General except on terms of absolute submission.

"This order was almost immediately followed by the replacement of Sherman by General Grant."

The Austrian envoy commented: "The attitude taken by the government in this case is highly significant, but not from a military viewpoint, since the war is decided by now. . . . This fact is significant in the sense that it is characteristic of the policy inaugurated by the new President: 'No transaction with the rebels, no quarter for their chiefs.' This seems to be the program of Mr. Andrew Johnson."

Wydenbruck thought that the new President's "excessive irritation" was, at least partly, caused by the fact that Sherman's leniency might have opened "an outlet for the escape of Jefferson Davis, on whose capture the new President sets great value. . . . "

Wydenbruck recalled that "on an analogous occasion, soon after Lee's surrender, Lincoln was asked instructions regarding Jefferson Davis, whose capture appeared imminent. Lincoln replied: 'One should shut his eyes.' . . . And in a similar spirit—although on a different topic—Lincoln replied to a foreigner who tried to sound him out on the Mexican question: 'I do not know,' said President Lincoln, 'what people will do, but what I know is that under my Presidency there will be no more wars.' "[2]

The Baron's view of President Johnson was seconded by Prince Metternich in Paris, who opined contemptuously: "Johnson, who succeeded Lincoln, is a demagogue who permits himself to be influenced by the mob."[3]

WYDENBRUCK'S REPORTS were increasingly pessimistic on Mexico. In his letter of April 18th he said that "the first effects of peace as far as Mexico is concerned" were a "military emigration," meaning the flight of detached Southern guerrillas, "who infest the country," across the border to Mexico. In contrast to some observers, Wydenbruck predicted that this unorganized "military emigration" would never establish contact with the imperial forces of Mexico and that only "the party of Juárez will profit therefrom."

The human flotsam of the once proud army of the South was, anyway, of little military value. For the most part they consisted of small bands of leaderless soldiers of the lower ranks who lived off the land and had no homes to return to. Driven over the border, they readily joined the Mexican guerrillas of Juárez even though the latter was an ally of the hated Yankees. But no questions were asked, and the hungry guerrillas were not interested in historical paradoxes.

There was, however, another flux of Southern refugees of the higher strata of the Confederacy which headed for the Mexican Empire and was welcomed by Maximilian. Soon after the surrender of the Confederate armies, the Mexican Emperor accepted a plan for colonization sub-

[2] Wydenbruck to Mensdorff-Pouilly, April 28, 1865.
[3] Metternich to Mensdorff-Pouilly, April 17, 1865.

mitted to him by the Confederate Commodore Matthew Fontaine Maury. The plan foresaw a systematic resettlement of a large number of Southern "gentlemen refugees" in Mexico, who were willing to offer their services to the Emperor rather than surrender to the Union. Hundreds of them fled at the close of the Civil War and established a "Southern" colony in the Córdoba region, among them Confederate Generals John Magruder, Joseph Shelby, Sterling Price, and political leaders such as the Governor of Louisiana, Henry W. Allen, and California Supreme Court Judge David S. Terry.[4]

Maury was, in addition to being a naval officer, a distinguished hydrographer and meteorologist and as such holder of a high Austrian decoration. "When Maximilian embarked upon his Mexican venture, Maury sent his warmest wishes for the success of his undertaking." [5] Maximilian was glad to welcome a prominent American at his court and in the summer of 1865 appointed him Imperial Commissioner of Emigration with Cabinet rank.

Maximilian, with characteristic enthusiasm, approved of Maury's large-scale colonization project and hoped it would become a new source of military and economic strength for his realm. There was no lack of mutual promises, and, among others, General Shelby vowed to "recruit forty thousand former Confederates" for the Emperor.[6] But again it was too late.

Before the year was over, Maximilian realized that his colonization policy provoked the anger of Washington, which wanted no "Confederacy in exile" south of the United States border. By October, 1865, Maximilian decided to cancel Maury's grand project, and the brief

[4] William Marshall Anderson's *Diaries,* edited by Ramón Eduardo Ruiz, The Huntington Library.
[5] *Ibid.*
[6] *Ibid.*

honeymoon between the Southern royalists and the Mexican Emperor was over.

ABRAHAM LINCOLN WAS resting in his grave at his home town of Springfield, Illinois, and Jefferson Davis was a captive in Georgia, when the Imperial Austrian government was still congratulating the dead President on the capture of Richmond.

Ten days after the assassination, the Foreign Minister of Francis Joseph, Count Mensdorff-Pouilly, wrote a letter to Baron Wydenbruck. His Excellency acknowledged the report on the fall of Richmond and the capitulation of General Lee, and said:

"These two big events, which may be considered as decisive for the conclusion of the war between the North and the South of the Republic of the United States"—how punctiliously correct the imperial phraseology has become —"were welcomed by the Imperial government with the keenest satisfaction."

And then the instructions which could no longer be carried out: "When you transmit the substance of this sentiment to President Lincoln, would you express to His Excellency our most sincere congratulations for these brilliant results. . . . "

True, the first transatlantic cable—one of the miracles of the mechanical age—was still one year short of completion, and Baron Wydenbruck had to send his reports by ship to Austrian consuls at Southampton, Queenstown, and Portsmouth, who would then transmit their gist by wire. But even so, steamships crossed the Atlantic in eight or nine days and sailing vessels in twelve to thirteen days. Baron Wydenbruck's first "telegram" on Lincoln's death arrived in Vienna on the twenty-eighth of April, which means that it was forwarded by the slowest boat available. Count Mensdorff-Pouilly's victory congratulation letter of April 24th was seemingly mailed in England on April 26th and possibly took two days longer to cross the Atlantic in the reverse direction. It should have reached the White House on May 12th or 13th, approximately one month after the assassination of Lincoln.

But then Austrian imperial bureaucrats were never in a hurry.

XIII

THE DIGNIFIED AND CALCI-fied slow-motion statecraft of Europe's *ancien régime* was thrown out of gear by the victory of Lincoln's America. The frightened empires began their final withdrawal from the Western Hemisphere, and their governments hastened to appease their respective home oppositions, emboldened by the triumph of the common man's Republic.

Napoleon III capitulated to Seward's energetic note in December, 1865, demanding immediate withdrawal of the French forces from Mexico. At home he rediscovered his liberal principles which he had conveniently forgotten during his imperialist-authoritarian period. His fervor for his Habsburg associates cooled and he decided to remain neutral in the increasingly bitter conflict between Austria and Prussia.

Maximilian tried desperately to bring about a *rap-*

prochement with the new President of the United States, but Andrew Johnson, like Lincoln before him, refused to receive his envoys or to read his letters. On one occasion Seward told Baron Wydenbruck pointedly that "Maximilian must leave Mexico." [1] To underline his Mexican policy, Johnson sent an army of fifty thousand under the command of General Sheridan to the Texas border. The hard-pressed Emperor of Mexico sent out an urgent call for help to his European colleagues and relatives—even to his hated brother, Francis Joseph. But to no avail.

Emperor Francis Joseph, under the pressure of his family and Maximilian's numerous adherents, did give orders to recruit volunteers on a large scale for Mexico. But a strong note from Seward sufficed to convince him that it would be foolhardy to let the volunteer army embark for the New World whose approaches were guarded by the mighty United States navy.

THE DECISION TO SACRIFICE his brother on the altar of political expediency seemed to be justified in the view of Francis Joseph by the situation in Europe. The struggle for German supremacy between Prussia and Austria was brought to a head by Prussian Premier (later Prince) Otto von Bismarck-Schoenhausen.[2] He involved Austria in a war against Denmark under the pretext of "liberating" the duchies of Schleswig and Holstein, but in reality to gain the important harbor of Kiel for the new Prussian navy. Since Austria prevented him from outright annexation of the duchies, Bismarck turned the modernized Prussian army against Francis Joseph's resplendent forces, which flaunted more tradition than firepower. In the Seven Weeks' War (summer, 1866), heavily industrialized Prussia defeated the largely agricultural Empire of Francis

[1] Wydenbruck to Mensdorff-Pouilly, February 13, 1866.
[2] Bismarck was Premier of Prussia 1862–90 and Chancellor of the German Empire 1871–90.

Joseph and expelled Austria from the German Confederation.

Francis Joseph was also forced to relinquish his grip over the province of Venetia and withdraw from United Italy. His military and political frustrations made him amenable to constitutional reforms, and he granted self-government to his republican-minded Hungarian subjects. His realm was transformed into the Austro-Hungarian Monarchy, a personal union with two independent governments and two parliaments. He was crowned Constitutional King of Hungary in 1867. By this compromise he prevented the outbreak of a new anti-Habsburg revolution—at least during his lifetime.

ENGLAND WAS REGARDED as having the most advanced political system of all Europe. Yet, in the middle of the nineteenth century, it was still a far cry from a democracy as we understand it today. The great majority of Britons had no representation in Parliament, and a few hundred feudal families dominated the political and social life of the country. During the American Civil War a mass movement of labor and the lower middle class demanded the vote with increasing vigor, and their leader, John Bright, hailed the Constitution of the great Republic across the sea as the ideal instrument of democracy. After the victory of the Union, the rulers of Britain quickly introduced a new parliamentary reform and granted the vote to millions of their America-inspired citizens.

This took place in 1867, the year when self-government was granted to Canada. The latter measure was intended to counteract the attraction of the triumphant Republic for the last British possession in North America. It was an open secret that Seward believed in an eventual, peaceful merger of Canada with the United States and that a great number of citizens in both American countries shared his hope. This belief was one of the principal reasons why Seward in 1867 purchased Russian-held Alaska for the "extravagant" sum of $7,200,000. Also, we may assume that England-hating Czar Alexander II and his wily Foreign Minister Prince Gorchakov were anxious to promote Seward's ambitions—and more trouble between England and America. This, probably, was their main motive in ceding their American real estate, outflanking Canada, to the United States.

ALL THESE WIDELY scattered but historically and emotionally linked developments were hastened by Lincoln's victory. Its repercussions, indeed, were felt all over the globe—as for instance in Japan, where the unique transformation of medieval Nippon into a modern industrial power was certainly influenced by American events. During the Civil War the feudal daimyos (nobles) of Japan still carried on their armed resistance against foreigners. But after the reunion of the United States they completely reversed their attitude. The daimyos' *coup d' état* of 1868, which ended the medieval Shogunate, heralded the beginning of the new era.

OF COURSE, the underlying cause of the great social and political changes that took place in the past century was the industrialization and urbanization of society. It demanded freedom of movement for the slaves, peons, and serfs, whose labor had sustained the large estates, and turned them into industrial workers. It called for freedom of enterprise for the bankers and industrialists of the middle classes who gradually superseded the landed aristocracy in controlling the affairs of the state. But the pace of history would have been slowed down if the Southern feudalists and their imperial backers had been successful in their anachronistic venture. Napoleon III would not have withdrawn his army from Mexico, Maximilian would have continued his conquistadorian role, Bismarck could not have maneuvered a victorious French Emperor into neutrality, and Francis Joseph would not have been isolated and humiliated by Prussia. Britain would have built up Canada as its military base in America, instead of granting it self-government, and the feudal system of Japan would possibly have gained a reprieve.

The last great effort of the *ancien régime*, however, collapsed with the victory of the Union, and Lincoln's name became synonymous with social progress all over the world. Lincoln was no theoretician. The closest thing to formulating the social idea with which he became identified was his epigram: "As I would not be a *slave*, so I would not be a *master*. This expresses my idea of democracy." [3]

Neither was Lincoln conscious that a new era had dawned in the political history of mankind as a result of his victory over the emperors. Yet the outcome of the Civil War marked a turn as great as any in the course of history: it was the principal cause of the fall of the Mexican and, somewhat later, the French Empires. It was one of the determining causes of the decline of the Austrian Empire and of the emergence of the United States as a world power.

EMPEROR MAXIMILIAN was aware of the rapidly increasing might of the re-United States and tried hard to improve his relations with Washington. Although his approaches had been steadfastly rejected, on August 4, 1865, he wrote another letter to President Johnson:

(A Spanish annotation states that it is a "Draft of a letter from the Emperor to the President of the United States.")

Far be it from me to give way to petty considerations [Maximilian here refers obviously to his previous rebuffs by Lincoln and Johnson] when my duties as a ruler are involved, and not for a minute do I hesitate to take the first step toward

[3] Fragment written by Lincoln in Springfield, Illinois, 1858.

the restoration of the friendly relations that had formerly ex-isted between the United States and Mexico. Since the hostile attitude of the greater part of the press in the United States and the strict reserve observed by your government toward the Mexican question are by no means helpful to the current process of regeneration and consolidation of the Mexican Em-pire, may I invite you in the friendliest spirit to enter into a personal correspondence with me regarding this important matter. This method, so I hope at least, will lead us more quickly and surely to our goal than protracted diplomatic negotiations.

Disregarding the superficial and biased view frequently expressed on the Mexican Empire by the United States press, I can see no valid reason why the powerful neighbor Republic should not, to our mutual advantage, desist from her opposi-tion to the Empire of Mexico, which is constructed on a similar basis and displays similar tendencies as the government of the United States. On the contrary, it appears to me that both states by their geographical situation and interests are predestined to join forces in pursuance of their common pur-pose to serve civilization and progress. Finding the sure and quick way (I believe) depends merely on the good will to come to an understanding between ourselves.

Those who are entitled to vote, that is the propertied and the working classes in the state, have chosen me to govern their destiny, and, besides the many difficulties involved, I did not hesitate for a single moment to follow their call—a task which I regard as my life's mission and which, with the help of God and all the power at my command, I am resolved to fulfill. Also, I am determined boldly to defy all the external complications which fate may bring. My immediate task, which I have continuously before my eyes, is to create con-ditions which would enable the peace-loving citizen to express his political opinion without fear of being exposed to partisan vengeance. As it is impossible to achieve this aim by peaceful means, it must be enforced by the might of arms. Ample reasons for these regrettable circumstances in Mexico can be found in the history of the country. Before we [in Mexico] can establish the liberal institutions which so advantageously distinguish the United States from other governmental systems, it is evident that we have to eliminate the mercenary party leaders and bandits who exploit the moral wretchedness and credulity of the people to the detriment of the whole country. They pursue only their private interests and—as shown by many examples in history—they are always ready to sell Freedom and Fatherland for their own benefit. For almost half a century the poor people have suffered under such outrageous oppression and, exhausted from the eternal civil wars, they were unable to get rid of their burden of their own accord. The cause I am representing could be rightfully considered as the common concern of the entire civilized world and the state which I am erecting is not intended to be an Empire on the European model, but a state of freedom and progress and the home of the most liberal institutions based on the same solid pillars as those of our mighty neighbor Republic. I have always been an admirer and ardent defender of its [American] principles, and my political past guarantees, above everything else, that I will apply those principles to the Mexican situation.

I am aware that the American press never tires of publishing malicious interpretations of events in this country—some even go so far as to throw suspicion on my good intentions. But, under the present circumstances in America and in view of the attitude of the European states toward the American Civil War, I could not expect a more favorable reception on the part of the press; however, you, President, are far too experienced to attach more weight to the press than it deserves. Indeed, I have understanding for a certain feeling of resentment on the part of the people of the United States, whose lofty self-respect was hurt by the intervention of the French army and its continued presence in this country. Yet, this took place only to serve the purpose of civilization—as a necessary measure which could not be avoided. The intervention will cease altogether as soon as it has fulfilled its mission.

The bearer of this letter is Consul General von Loosey, who is known to you through his many years' residence in the United States. Mr. Loosey enjoys my full confidence and is familiar with my ideas and, therefore, he is in a position —even more than my letter would be—to give you all information concerning this matter.

Hoping, President, that our correspondence will not end with this letter and that I shall, in the very near future, have an opportunity to confer with you, in writing or orally, on this important matter, I am,

Your, etc.

Consul General von Loosey had no more luck than his Mexican predecessor. Maximilian's letter was not even read by Johnson, and Herr von Loosey was granted no audience. Maximilian was rebuffed by his strongest adversary and was soon to be abandoned by his closest ally.

THE SUDDEN SHIFT in the power balance of the world was reflected in Napoleon's changed attitude. The erstwhile leader of the royal conspiracy against Lincoln's Republic, who had invaded Mexico, defied the Monroe Doctrine, supported the Confederacy, tried to colonize parts of Mexico and the United States (Sonora and Texas), was, after the conclusion of the Civil War, attempting to appease Washington with proposals of territorial concessions. In fact, he offered the protectorate of Mexico—formerly his greatest ambition—to the United States.

It was in October, 1865, that Napoleon had approached Washington with the promise of withdrawal of all French forces from Mexico in exchange for recognition of Maximilian's Empire by the United States. His suggestion was rejected, and Seward in a sharp note demanded the unconditional evacuation of Mexico. When Napoleon realized that he would not be able to save the throne of his satrap Maximilian, he made a new offer to Washington.

Austrian envoy Baron Wydenbruck reported a year later, in October, 1866, to Count Mensdorff-Pouilly that

"France offered immediate evacuation *and* the cession of two Mexican provinces, Lower California and Sonora, contiguous to United States territory, *provided* America, by virtue of the protectorate, which it is to exercise over Mexico, would guarantee French interests in these countries."

The Austrian envoy found it hard to believe this complete turnabout of the French Emperor and qualified his information as an unconfirmed rumor. However, in a secret memorandum to his wife, Empress Carlota,[4] Maximilian himself furnished the confirmation that territorial concessions to the United States were seriously considered in exchange for consolidating his Empire "as the central power in the new continent." The Mexican Emperor was willing to cede certain northern districts of his country to the United States, provided Washington would agree to a division of the Western Hemisphere into three spheres of influence: domination by the United States in the north, by the Mexican Empire in the center, and by the Empire of Brazil in the south.

But Seward and President Johnson refused to deal with the "Austrian adventurer"—as Maximilian was dubbed in Washington at the time—and ridiculed the idea of taking over the protectorate of the unwanted Mexican Empire from their archenemy, Napoleon III. Seward's answer to Napoleon's approaches was an ultimatum to get out of Mexico.

MAXIMILIAN'S SITUATION became increasingly desperate. He, who had arrived to be the arbiter of the New World, had to give up even the idea of sharing its domination with other powers. Frustrated to the point of hopelessness, Maximilian gave serious thought to withdrawing as gracefully as possible from his strife-torn Empire and, forgetting his wounded pride, made a

[4] November 6, 1865.

last approach to President Johnson, whom he addressed, this time in English, as "My great and good friend":

I herewith send Your Excellency copies of a proclamation which I have today adressed to the Mexican nation, as well as of the laws which form the completion of it; the object of the one, as well as the other is to prevent further bloodshed and to put an end to a war, which threatens to end only with the destruction of the entire country, filling my heart with the most profound grief.

I have accordingly not hesitated to appeal to the good sense of the whole people of Mexico calling upon them to elect freely and without obstacle whatsoever a national Congress, based on the principle of universal suffrage, who is to decide on the future form of Government. *Should that body determine upon any other form than the monarchical, I am ready to deliver the power which I hold, into the hands of that body and to retire from the headship of a government which I have accepted only because I was made to understand that such was the wish and the will of a majority of the people of Mexico:* a position which certainly offers no other inducement except the hope of being enabled to accomplish the happiness and wellfare of Mexico. [Italics are the author's.]

I have appealed, as Your Excellency will perceive from the content of the documents to the several chiefs of the republican army to lay down their arms until the assemblage of the Deputies and the decision of the principal question; the main object of the present letter is to ask Your Excellency's good interference and influence to obtain the adhesion of those chiefs to the invitation which I have directed to them, and the acceptance of which will at once enable the people of Mexico to determine upon the principal question which are being agitated and to select the rulers most acceptable to them.

To this decision none will subject with greater cheerfullness, nor bow to their selection with more sincere gratification than myself.

I cannot bring my mind to the belief that Your Excellency will hesitate for a moment to aid in this manner to bring to a termination the unhappy struggle which has divided Mexico during the past years and to give it a last oportunity of organizing a stable government which may satisfy its wants and necesities and lead it to glory and prosperity.[5]

Johnson, however, once more declined to accept Maximilian's letter, and Seward's indirect answer—sent via Paris —was: Get out of Mexico.

EVEN EMPRESS EUGÉNIE, that master-intrigante behind the scenes, realized the inevitability of capitulation in view of the overwhelming might of the United States. But she blamed her imperial husband for having missed the great opportunity of consolidating the Mexican Empire before the fall of the Confederacy and urged him to retrieve France's military prestige by a new war. She advocated a close military alliance with the Austrian Empire and a preventive war against Prussia. When she saw the futility of her efforts, she accused Napoleon of mental and physical infirmity.

At the height of her desperation she demanded that the Emperor "should disappear from the political scene for a while"—euphemism for abdication—and let a regency, under her own guidance, grasp the reins of France.

After the battle of Koeniggraetz, where Bismarck's lightning attack smashed the Austrian army, Eugénie confided to Prince Metternich: "I have done all that is humanly possible but . . . I am almost alone in my beliefs." She was alone because she was blamed by all, even her former co-conspirators, for the ill-fated Mexican adventure.

Metternich faithfully reported Empress Eugénie's confidences to Vienna—among others, her premonition: "France is on her road to ruin." [6]

The downfall of the Second Empire had been sealed by the victory of Lincoln's America.

[5] Draft of letter sent late 1866.
[6] Metternich to Mensdorff-Pouilly, July 11 and July 26, 1866.

XIV

THE FIRST OF THE THREE Emperors who followed Lincoln to where all social struggles cease was Maximilian of Mexico. His death was no less tragic than that of Abraham Lincoln; the Emperor was executed by revolutionaries. But Lincoln died in his hour of triumph, as happy as achievement of his supreme goal could make a man. Maximilian went down with his whole world crumbling, his Empire lost, his trust betrayed, his wife insane, his friends deserting, and his last two faithful generals facing the execution squad with him.

He was aware of the approaching catastrophe and tried to fight it. He knew that all was lost and tried to escape his doom. But he was too weak to succeed and too proud to flee. Only two weeks after the assassination of Lincoln, when he was still writing condolences to President Johnson, Emperor Maximilian on April 30th sent an urgent request to Napoleon to appeal to all "interested powers" for a joint declaration against the aggressive policy of the United States. "The events taking place at our northern frontier," wrote Maximilian, "and those occurring within the United States have become so serious that my people must be officially notified of the support of the European powers, upon which I am counting."

Napoleon ignored the request, sent to him by a special envoy, and Empress Eugénie observed that Maximilian was "prone to ask for impossible things." Meanwhile, Washington with increasing emphasis urged the withdrawal of the French army from Mexico, and on January 15, 1866, Napoleon informed Maximilian "not without painful emotion" that he was forced to "fix a definite time limit" to the occupation of Mexico.

Maximilian answered with bitter irony that "I am too much a friend of yours to desire to be the direct or indirect cause of any danger to Your Majesty. . . ." At the same time, he reminded Napoleon of his solemn promises and their treaties.

Napoleon's reply was twofold. On April 5th, his official *Moniteur* announced that the evacuation of Mexico would begin in the fall of 1866 and would be completed a year later. And he wrote to Maximilian rather coolly that "it would be impossible for me to ask the *Corps Législatif* for new sacrifices." [1]

MAXIMILIAN AND CARLOTA now realized the extreme peril threatening their throne and even their lives. The withdrawal of Marshal Bazaine's army would deprive their Empire of the strongest, best-equipped, battle-trained troops. There was no love lost between Maximilian and Bazaine, who, behind the scenes, were constantly

[1] Letters exchanged between Napoleon and Maximilian, January 15, February 18, and April 12, 1866.

competing for power and prestige. But Bazaine was the only commander in Mexico who had the means and the ability to "pacify" the country. Moreover, Napoleon's armed support was the only protection Maximilian had against the overwhelming might of the United States. Nothing but the certainty of involvement in war with France seemed to have prevented direct intervention on the part of Mexico's northern neighbor, who was already concentrating troops on its frontier. There was no hope of changing Napoleon's mind, and Empress Eugénie was obviously not willing to interfere. And King Leopold of Belgium had died at the end of 1865.

The corrupt but influential Morny clique disintegrated and its head, the Duke of Morny, died earlier in the year —even before he could collect his share of the notorious Jecker loan. So, payment of 12,660,000 francs by Maximilian's treasury for the 3,375,000 francs which banker Jecker had advanced to the conservative Miramón government helped no one except Jecker himself. The Mexican treasury was empty, the large landowners and the property-tied middle class sabotaged taxation, and the lower classes were openly hostile to the imperial regime.

Maximilian's halfhearted attempt to recruit a fresh army in Austria was foiled by the quick action of Seward. The Secretary of State instructed his envoy at Vienna, Mr. Motley, to protest against sending any "volunteers" to Mexico and should his protest go unheeded to ask for his passport and return to Washington. Seward indicated that further armed help to Maximilian would provoke a state of war between the United States and Austria.[2]

This put an irrevocable end to Francis Joseph's never too enthusiastic efforts to help his brother Maximilian. Carlota's brother, the new King of Belgium, followed the lead of the French and Austrian Emperors and flatly re-

[2] Wydenbruck to Mensdorff-Pouilly, April 25, 1866.

fused help. In their extreme predicament the imperial couple decided that Empress Carlota should go to Europe and plead personally with Napoleon III and Pope Pius IX.

CARLOTA EMBARKED for France in July, 1866, resolved to remind Napoleon and Eugénie of their promises and treaty obligations. Were not the French sovereigns chiefly responsible for the Mexican enterprise? Had not the compact between Napoleon and Maximilian stipulated that "irrespective of the turn of events in Europe, the assistance of France shall never fail the new Empire"? [3] But the reception in Paris was cool and disappointing. Carlota was not treated as an honored guest of the imperial couple, and was not invited to stay at the palace. In fact, Empress Eugénie disclosed to her that the Emperor was too ill to receive her at all.

Humiliated and desperate, Carlota lost her royal bearings. After a hysterical scene, Eugénie promised to get her an audience with the Emperor. Napoleon tried to teach her a lesson in practical politics, but Carlota was unreceptive and, amid tears and shouts, hurled invectives at him. Napoleon subsequently informed Maximilian on August 29th of the encounter, saying that he had received Empress Carlota "with great pleasure" but "it was painful for me to be unable to accede to the request she had submitted to me."

Carlota left Paris in a fury and went to Rome. Pope Pius IX probably looked forward to meeting Carlota with the same "pleasure" as did Napoleon, but he received the unhappy Empress of Mexico on September 27th. She besought the Pontiff to induce Napoleon to change his mind and to appeal to all Catholic monarchs to go to the aid of Maximilian. Had not the Pope encouraged her husband to accept the crown of Mexico and to restore the privilege of the Church in that revolution-torn country?

Pius IX offered her his blessing but no help. Carlota

[3] Napoleon to Maximilian, Miramar Convention, April 10, 1864.

left the Vatican in a despondent mood, only to return and demand to see the Pope once more. She accused members of her escort of being hirelings of Napoleon trying to poison her. She saw an assassin in every corner, behind every column, and pleaded for asylum. On the steps of the Vatican the Empress of Mexico collapsed amid unmistakable signs of persecution mania.[4]

THE NEWS OF THE tragic end of his wife's mission broke the pride of Maximilian. He at last agreed to leave his capital, already threatened by the growing armies of Juárez. In October, 1866, Emperor Maximilian fled to Orizaba and sent his archives with some personal belongings to his frigate *Novara*, which was prepared for any emergency in the harbor of Veracruz. But he rejected Marshal Bazaine's demand to abdicate before returning to Europe under French protection.[5] He refused to give Napoleon and Bazaine the satisfaction of rescuing him and possibly using him as a scapegoat.

His Mexican generals, Miramón and Mejia, pleaded with him not to desert them and the royalists of Mexico. After long hesitation Maximilian returned, assumed personal command of the few loyal troops, and in February, 1867, set up his headquarters in the walled city of Querétaro. It was a suicidal resolve. After a few months' hopeless resistance, the besieged city fell and the Emperor was captured. No pleas for mercy, not even Seward's intervention, could prevail upon Juárez to show leniency. Seward's telegram was dispatched on April 6, 1867, by Military Telegraph to L. D. Campbell, United States minister to Mexico, then in New Orleans, Louisiana:

"The capture of the Prince Maximilian in Querétaro

[4] Official Reports of Dr. Jilek, Count Bombelles, and von Radonetz, October 1, 1866.

[5] Wydenbruck to the new Austrian Foreign Minister, Baron (later Count) Friedrich Ferdinand von Beust, November 20, 1866.

by the Republican armies of Mexico, seems probable. The reported severity practiced upon the prisoners at Zacatecas excites apprehensions that similar severity may be practiced in the case of the Prince and his alien troops. Such severities would be injurious to the national cause of Mexico and to the Republican system throughout the world.

"You will communicate to President Juárez, promptly and by effectual means, the desire of this Government that in case of capture, the Prince and his supporters may receive humane treatment accorded by civilized nations to Prisoners of war."

But Juárez insisted that "the foreign usurper" who had put his signature under the decree outlawing all republicans was responsible for the summary execution of many of his followers. Maximilian was sentenced to death by a court-martial and executed by a firing squad at Querétaro on June 19, 1867. His last two faithful generals, Miramón and Mejia, were shot alongside their Emperor.

MEANWHILE AN EX-GENERAL of the former Confederate states had galloped to the rescue of the two beaten Habsburg Emperors, Francis Joseph of Austria and Maximilian of Mexico. This unexpected help is indicated in Baron Wydenbruck's interesting report to Count Mensdorff-Pouilly of August 20, 1866:

My Lord,

Your Excellency will have been informed by the Imperial Legation in Mexico that the Mexican city of Matamoros, situated on the right bank of the Rio Grande, after having withstood a long siege under the command of General Mejia, surrendered to the Juárists under the condition that the garrison would be peacefully withdrawn; and that immediately thereafter this city was declared in a state of blockade by the Imperial Government of Mexico. By decree of the seventeenth of the month, the President of the United States has just declared that, owing to the insufficiency of forces which blockade Matamoros, this blockade could not be considered effective, and that therefore any attempt to enforce it in connection with the maritime commerce of the United States will not be tolerated, i.e., it "should be disallowed." [6] I have the honor of enclosing herewith the text of the decree.

The Convention of the conservative or Democratic party, as I had the honor of informing Your Excellency in advance, took place in Philadelphia the fourteenth of this month instead of on the day previously fixed. The purpose of the resolutions which have been adopted as the platform of the Convention was to influence the elections now in progress for the new Congress. The principal points of the platform are: the restoration of the rights of Sovereignty (state rights) to each of the states of the Union and the denial of the right usurped by the Congress of excluding, as has been done up to now, the representatives of the Southern states. The Convention closed with a vote of confidence in President Johnson, assuring him of the support of the Convention. As Mr. Johnson is notoriously the author and the promoter of the Convention of Philadelphia, the platform adopted ought to be considered as a new declaration of principles to the nation on his behalf. Generally it is doubted that the Convention has produced the effect hoped for by its author, and that the conservative (Democratic) party may succeed in restoring its old supremacy.

On the twenty-eighth of this month the President, accompanied by Mr. Seward and other high functionaries, will make a tour in the North of the country. The ostensible purpose of his trip is to attend the ceremony of laying the foundation stone of a monument which the city of Chicago is erecting. In reality, Mr. Johnson's intention is to visit the principal Northern cities to make speeches there and prepare his vote-getting campaign for his re-election to the Presidency in 1869 [sic].

The five large military divisions of the United States are

[6] According to the Declaration of Paris, suscribed to by the principal maritime powers, a blockade must be "effective" to be recognized by the nonbelligerent governments. Maximilian's navy was far from being "effective."

going to be discontinued. Henceforth all of the territory will be divided in eleven (11) military departments. The troubles which broke out in New Orleans July 29th, and of which I had the honor of giving an account to Your Excellency, have not recurred. It has not been judged expedient to suspend the martial law which General Sheridan proclaimed following the events which took place in that city.

It remains for me to mention a letter which I received, several days ago, from General Anderson, of the old Confederate army, who, in view of the war between Austria and Prussia, expresses the desire of entering our army and offering to raise, among his old comrades-in-arms, a corps of five thousand men for the service of His Majesty the Emperor. [Italics are the author's.] However, in principle, the recruiting of a military corps in America on behalf of Austria may not be feasible because of the [American] laws pertaining to neutrality. And, even if this were not the case, the approaching re-establishment of peace deprives General Anderson's proposition of its timeliness. Nevertheless, I believe that Your Excellency should not be kept in ignorance of this matter. I wonder if there would be a way for the Mexican Empire to take advantage of the good will of General Anderson.

Please deign to accept, My Lord, my deep respect.

WYDENBRUCK

The Austrian envoy did not identify further the last undaunted monarchist of the South, and there were three General Andersons who could qualify: Lieutenant General Richard Henry Anderson, Major General James Patton Anderson, and Brigadier General George Thomas Anderson.

Evidently Wydenbruck treated General Anderson with respect and took his offer seriously. However, the Austro-Prussian war lasted only a few weeks, and troop reinforcements were no longer needed by the Emperor. Yet, the Baron ventured the suggestion "I wonder if there would be a way for the Mexican Empire to take advantage of the good will of General Anderson."

Emperor Francis Joseph, however, knew when he was beaten, and after the catastrophic defeat of Koeniggraetz by the Prussians, he had no intention of challenging the United States by accepting the renegade American General's offer. The Austrian Foreign Minister Count Mensdorff-Pouilly instructed his Washington envoy to decline the assistance of the doughty Confederate warrior:

To Baron Wydenbruck
   Washington
Vienna, September 10, 1866

In the report of August 20th, that I had the honor of receiving from you, mention is made of the desire expressed by General Anderson, of the old Confederate army, of joining the imperial army [of Austria] and of recruiting a corps of five thousand men from among his old comrades-in-arms for the service of His Majesty the Emperor in the war between Austria and Prussia.

Although, as you remarked, the neutrality laws in force in the United States of America and, on the other hand, the re-establishment of peace deprives Mr. Anderson's proposition of its expediency, the imperial government has no less appreciated the interest of the General and the good will evinced on this occasion, and I ask you, Baron, to convey and interpret this sentiment to him.

As far as Mexico is concerned, an offer similar to that made by the General—assuming that it were realizable and beneficial to the cause of the Mexican Empire—would by its very nature aggravate the already quite difficult position of that Empire vis-à-vis the United States.

Receive . . .
(Initialed by Imperial Foreign Minister
Count Mensdorff-Pouilly)

XV

NAPOLEON III AND HIS SEC-
ond Empire could not sur-
vive the total defeat of his costly American enterprise for
any length of time. His army of conquest decimated, his
treasury and arsenals emptied, his prestige at home and
abroad at an all-time low, he was an easy prey for rising
Prussia's ambitions. Aware of his own weakness, he quickly
acceded to Bismarck's request to maintain neutrality during
the Austro-Prussian conflict, and hoped to profit from
what he expected to be a prolonged war between the two
powers.

The lightning attack of the Prussians, however, upset
Napoleon's calculations, and within a few weeks he saw
Austria decisively defeated. France now faced a tremen-
dously strengthened Prussia while Austria was lost as a
potential ally. Bismarck's next step toward securing Prussian
hegemony on the continent of Europe was to isolate and

challenge France. Napoleon, of course, presented Bismarck with a bill for his neutrality, asking for territorial concessions at the expense of Bavaria, Belgium, or Luxembourg. The French demands—inspired by Bismarck himself in his prewar talks with Napoleon—were shrewdly divulged by Bismarck. This stratagem had the desired effect of turning these potentially pro-French countries against France and arousing latent suspicions in Britain. Italy joined the Prussian camp in return for Bismarck's promise to help United Italy to recover the province of Venetia from Austria. In addition Italy was pledged Protestant Prussia's support in its efforts to annex Rome, which at the time was still under Papal sovereignty by the grace of God and Napoleon's troops.

The Franco-Prussian War broke out in July, 1870, and proved to be another lightning victory. The French army commanded by Napoleon was routed at Sedan on September 1st, and the Emperor himself was captured. Marshal Bazaine, who commanded the pivotal defense group based on the fortifications of Metz, surrendered on October 27th with an army of 170,000. After the war Bazaine was condemned for treason for his capitulation, but with the help of his Mexican wife he escaped to Spain.

With the Peace of Versailles, signed on January 18, 1871, the war was practically over. Only Paris defied the siege of the Prussians and the new French government of Adolphe Thiers established at Versailles. Thiers, an Orléanist statesman, opposed Napoleon III. After the Emperor's fall, he headed the provisional government and made peace with the Prussian invaders. The Commune of Paris held out until the end of May, when it was finally defeated by forces of the Thiers government amid terrible violence and bloodshed. Triumphant Bismarck ordered his army to stand by, while the Rightist troops of Thiers suppressed the defiant Left. Indeed, the Paris Commune became the first of a series of European civil wars in which organized industrial workers played a prominent role. This signified a new phase of the Industrial Revolution, which had created the socialist movements and labor unions to counterbalance its first-born offspring, the financial and industrial giants, the trusts, cartels, and monopolies.

While tens of thousands were massacred in Paris, Napoleon went into exile in England, where he died two years later. Eugénie, whose life and jewels were saved by the Metternichs, survived him by almost half a century. She died in 1920 at ninety-four, blind, bitter, and perhaps envying Carlota, who reached old age in mental blindness, unhaunted by memories.

THUS THE THREE EMPERORS who had joined their might to reintroduce monarchy in America met their defeat separately, each watching the other go down without offering assistance.

Francis Joseph I did not go down all the way. He had been expelled from the German Federation, which, after the collapse of Napoleonic France, was transformed by Bismarck at Versailles into the German Empire under William I, King of Prussia. Austria lost the province of Venetia to Italy, but Bismarck had no intention of destroying the Austrian Empire. The "Iron Chancellor," a Prussian Junker to the marrow of his bones, had great sympathy for the landed aristocracy which dominated the Habsburg realm and was resolved to perpetuate the *ancien régime* in Central Europe.

Bismarck continued to rule until William I's grandson, William II—just as domineering as Bismarck—dismissed the latter in 1890 at the beginning of his reign. But Francis Joseph and his Empire got another lease on life and, after introducing far-reaching constitutional reforms, survived as the Austro-Hungarian Monarchy until the end of the First World War.

Despite the defeats of his armies, Francis Joseph continued to base his regime on his military and civil bureaucracy, which was officered by the aristocracy. But he became a constitutional monarch with a debilitated voice in internal as well as international affairs. His personal life was beset by tragedies: his only son, Crown Prince Rudolf, died in a double suicide with his mistress, Baroness Maria Vetsera, at the Mayerling hunting lodge in 1889. Nine years later his wife, Empress Elizabeth, was slain by an Italian anarchist in Geneva. His great-nephew, Archduke Francis Ferdinand, next in succession, was assassinated with his wife by a Serbian nationalist at Sarajevo,[1] touching off World War I. Francis Joseph died in 1916, and two years later—only slightly more than fifty years after the American Civil War—the Habsburg Empire disintegrated forever.

WHILE UNION VICTORY in the American Civil War was the direct or indirect cause of the decline of the Mexican, French, and Austrian Empires, by an ironic turn of history it contributed to the birth of a new German Empire. Bismarck's personal sympathies were, of course, with the large land- and slave-holders of the South—as he confided years later to Carl Schurz—but he was determined to exploit the Napoleonic-Habsburg adventure for his own political purposes. He opposed, therefore, recognition of the Confederacy and in return profited from the victory of the Union and the bloodletting of France in Mexico.

In the long run, however, the triumph of Lincoln's Republic had no less influence on Germany than on other countries. The attraction of the United States with its personal freedom and unrivaled economic possibilities was reflected by the increasing immigration from Europe, which in the year following the Civil War jumped to 318,000, to 669,000 fifteen years later, and which early in the twentieth century reached an annual average of 1,000,000—up to the

[1] June 28, 1914.

161

outbreak of the First World War. When the German Empire collapsed at the end of that war, the Constitution of the new German Republic was drawn along the lines of the American Constitution. This followed the trend then prevailing in most European countries—except in Russia.

IN THE VAST EMPIRE of the Czars, the progress of the Industrial Revolution was slower and the resistance of the *ancien régime* stronger than in any other country of Europe. Czar Alexander II, who during the Civil War supported the Union in order to harass England and France, had become embroiled in a feud with his own landed aristocracy when in 1861 he signed the ukase to emancipate the 23,000,000 serfs of Russia. The Czar's liberal inclinations, however, were soon stifled in the tense political atmosphere following a revolution of the Poles, which was bloodily suppressed. Six attempts were made on Alexander's life by the various extremist groups until a nihilist bomb killed him on March 13, 1881.

Under his successors Russia became more than ever a police state. The emancipation of the serfs failed to produce a landowning peasantry, and the medieval prerogatives of the *ancien régime* were maintained to a large extent in the autocratic Czarist state. But the Industrial Revolution could not forever be excluded from Russia, and the resulting anachronisms produced an inner weakness which was strikingly revealed by the Russo-Japanese War (1904-5) and the simultaneous uprisings within the Czarist Empire. The widespread rebellion—a prelude to the Revolution of 1917—was partly cruelly suppressed, partly appeased by the establishment of the Duma (Parliament), but the liberalization of Holy Russia was only of short duration. The war ended in a defeat of the Czarist army and navy, inflicted by the vastly underrated Japanese forces, and soon after the war the Russian opposition was again driven underground.

The big explosion came toward the end of World War I when military reverses, widespread corruption, and inefficiency in all branches of the administration, except the secret police, created an almost universal discontent. Leaders of the February Revolution (1917) aimed at an America-inspired constitution, but the moderate Kerensky government was unable to halt the impelling force of the long-suppressed revolution. Torn by internal dissensions and attacked by left and right, the Kerensky government was overthrown by Lenin's dedicated Communists in the October Revolution of the same year. This was followed by three years of devastating civil war, aggravated by mass starvation and foreign intervention. Under such circumstances only one of the two extremes could prevail: the survivor was the Communist regime, which gave land to the peasants, bread and arms to the workers, and dangled world revolution before the eyes of the faithful.

Soon after its great victory over its enemies, the insatiable Soviet Revolution started to devour its own children. The Stalin era began.

UNDER THE IMPACT of World War I and the ensuing revolutions all European Empires collapsed—all except the British Empire. It still controlled nearly one quarter of the globe, and had an economic solidity and political elasticity which absorbed the shock of the social changes generated by the Industrial Revolution. It became the prototype of a constitutional monarchy, where the sovereign is a decorative but lifeless political instrument in the hands of a parliamentary government. Its *ancien régime* gradually relinquished its constitutional privileges only to retain much of its political power by salvaging a considerable part of its social prominence. It evolved a genius of compromise, bestowing peerage on labor leaders and regilding its faded escutcheons with the dowries of American heiresses. On the other hand, the first labor unions in Europe were formed in England, and Karl Marx's First Socialist International was established in London as early as 1864.

Later, the British genius of compromise transformed the outdated Empire into a Commonwealth of Nations and managed to hold it together—although some of its members had revolted against British authority, had become independent, and, like India, adopted a republican constitution.

YET, THE BRITISH EMPIRE and its allies, deserted by Russia, might have lost World War I save for the entrance of the United States into the war. Although most Americans failed to realize it, the wheel of history had turned full circle since the Civil War. Lincoln's victory had secured America's continental unity and started her on the road from isolationism to interventionism. The Civil War, it turned out, was fought as much against Europe's Emperors, who were conspiring to establish their protectorate over North America, as against the feudal slaveholders of the South. In World War I, American intervention was provoked by the German imperial government's decision to wage unrestricted submarine warfare. This would have isolated the United States, which—although a policy of interventionism was certainly not in Lincoln's mind—had acquired a vested interest in the world seas.

But for the overwhelming majority of Europeans on both sides of the bloodstained front, the United States was still Abraham Lincoln's America, symbol of the long struggle against national and social oppression. President Woodrow Wilson's declaration that "the world must be made safe for democracy" and his subsequent "Fourteen Points" were hailed by all the peoples who overthrew their Emperors, from Kaiser Wilhelm II to the Sultan of Turkey.

At the end of World War I, when President Wilson went to the Peace Conference as a "champion of the rights of mankind," he was greeted as a messiah all over Europe. America's prestige during this decade was unparalleled, and even Sun Yat-sen, leader of the Chinese Revolution which began in 1911, looked to the United States as an inspiration in shaping his new Republic.

THE BRIEF REVIVAL of isolationism in the United States prevented American participation in the League of Nations—created by President Wilson—but it could not change the course of history. It would be impossible, in the frame of this Epilogue, to describe the political and economic developments which led to World War II. It should suffice to say briefly that World War I, which impoverished Europe, made America the creditor of the whole world. This has extended her vested interests in all continents and changed her political relations to governments and peoples. Resentment against the now richest country of the globe was also stirred by the imitation emperors who arose during the Fascist-Nazi reaction following the revolutionary period in Europe. The attempt of this counterrevolution to force upon Europe a medieval caste society, under the dictatorship of a military oligarchy, was the immediate cause of World War II. Once more American intervention became inevitable, and President Franklin D. Roosevelt emerged as the leader of the grand coalition confronting Adolf Hitler's Third Reich and its satellites.

Most European members of the new American-led coalition had been overrun by Hitler's legions and were engaged in a savage—mostly underground—civil war. The United States once again was hailed as the champion of the oppressed and the hope of the revolution in Europe. By the end of World War II, the United States—which less than a century before had escaped the fate of becoming a European protectorate—saw itself in the role of a protector of Western Europe.

This role was not deliberately sought by the United States. It was brought about by the political, economic, and military vacuum created by the Nazi havoc and the subsequent collapse of the Third Reich. The new authorities and the re-emerging industries in the Western half of Europe were entirely dependent on American support. A similar situation, left in the wake of the defeated Nazi armies, enabled Stalin's Russia to establish its own protectorate over most of Eastern Europe.

Thus, the semi-Asian Soviet Union and the American Republic have become the heirs to the power of the defunct European empires. Their rivalry has generated a new armaments race—and, thanks to our atomic age, more than one world is now beckoning to missile-equipped protectors.

THE ECSTASY OF WAR, civil war and revolution, so pessimists claim, is a permanent feature of human history. The atomic phase of the Industrial Revolution, they say, threatens to paraphrase the American motto "War to end war" into "War to end man." Optimists, on the other hand, insist that the very danger of an atomic war is likely to tame the political animal, reduce his armed contests to an absurdity and/or induce him to conquer other planets before destroying his own.

Were it possible for Abraham Lincoln to comment on the new problems and perils confronting America and mankind, he would probably quote his favorite "Oriental aphorism," which, he said, "is true and appropriate at all times and situations:

"'And this too shall pass away.'" [2]

[2] From an address at Milwaukee, Wisconsin, September 30, 1859.

Selected Bibliography

Lincoln and the Emperors is based principally on documents deposited in the Austrian State Archives. All diplomatic reports and correspondence not otherwise identified come from this primary source of information. Much of the source material is new, and those documents published previously were, to my best knowledge, never used in connection with the American Civil War. A few documents missing from the Archives, owing to wartime damage or dislocation, had to be replaced by copies of the originals. Two of these copies were found in the Library of Congress, Washington.

A complete list of the literature perused in the preparation of this book would include hundreds, or even thousands, of items. It seems inevitable to confine the bibliography to the most relevant books and other sources.

Adams, Charles Francis, 2nd, *Charles Francis Adams, by His Son* (1900).

Adams, E. D., *Great Britain and the American Civil War* (1925).

Anderson, William Marshall, *An American in Maximilian's Mexico* (1865-66). See also Ruiz, R. E.

Atkins, John Black, *The Life of Sir William Howard Russell* (1911).

Aubry, Octave, *The Second Empire* (1938).

Bailey, Thomas A., *A Diplomatic History of the American People* (1955).

Bancroft, Frederick, *Life of William H. Seward* (1900).

Beale, Howard K., *The Critical Year* (1930).

Beard, Charles A., *A Century of Progress: 1833-1933* (1933).

—— and Mary R., *The Rise of American Civilization* (1927).

Bell, Herbert C. F., *Lord Palmerston* (1936).

Bemis, Samuel Flagg, *Guide to the Diplomatic History of the United States* (1955).

Bigelow, John, *Retrospections of an Active Life* (1909-13).

——, *France and the Confederate Navy* (1888).

——, *Lest We Forget: Gladstone, Morley and the Confederate Loan of 1863* (1905).

Bruckberger, Raymond L., *America: The Revolution of Our Century* (1960).

Bulloch, James D., *Secret Service of the Confederate States in Europe* (1883). Revised edition (1960) by P. V. D. Stern.

Callahan, J. M., *Diplomatic Relations of the Confederate States with England* (1898).

Catton, Bruce, *Mr. Lincoln's Army* (1951).

——, *Glory Road* (1952).

——, *A Stillness at Appomattox* (1953).

——, *This Hallowed Ground* (1956).

——, *Grant Moves South* (1960).

Chambrun, Charles Adolphe, Marquis de, *Impressions of Lincoln and the Civil War* (1952).

Chase, Salmon P., *Diary and Correspondence* (1903).

Claussen, Martin P., *Peace Factors in Anglo-American Relations, 1861-1865* (1940).

Congressional Record, 31st Congress, Senate.

Corti, Conte Egon Caesar, *Maximilian and Charlotte of Mexico* (1929).

Current, Richard N. See J. G. Randall.

Dana, Charles A., *Lincoln and His Cabinet* (1899).

——, *Recollections of the Civil War* (1899).

Dana, Richard Henry, "The Trent Affair," *Proceedings, Massachusetts Historical Society*, Vol. XLV (1935).

Davis, Jefferson, *Rise and Fall of the Confederate Government* (1881).

Dennett, Tyler, *Lincoln and the Civil War in the Diaries and Letters of John Hay* (1939).

Dictionary of American Biography.

Donald, David, *Inside Lincoln's Cabinet: the Civil War Diaries of Salmon Portland Chase* (1954).

Eisenschiml, Otto, and Ralph Newman, *The American Iliad: The Epic Story of the Civil War* (1947).

Eisenschiml, Otto, and E. B. Long, *As Luck Would Have It: Chance and Coincidence in the Civil War* (1948).

Eisenschiml, Otto, *Addenda to Lincoln's Assassination* (1950).

Fleury, Maurice, Comte de, *Memoirs of the Empress Eugenie* (1920).

Foster, Genevieve, *Abraham Lincoln: An Initial Biography* (1950).

Fuess, Claude Moore, *Carl Schurz, Reformer* (1932).

Golder, Frank A., "The American Civil War Through the Eyes of a Russian Diplomat," *The American Historical Review*, Vol. 26 (1921).

Grant, U. S., *Personal Memoirs* (1885).

Greeley, Horace, *The American Conflict* (1869).

Guedalla, Philip, *Palmerston* (1926).

——, *The Second Empire* (1922).

Gurowski, Adam, *Diary* (1862-66).

Harnsberger, Caroline Thomas, *The Lincoln Treasury* (1950).

Harper's Weekly (1861-65).

Hendrick, Burton J., *Statesmen of the Lost Cause* (1939).
——, *Lincoln's War Cabinet* (1946).
Herndon, William H., and Jesse William Weik, *Herndon's Lincoln* (1889).
Howe, Mark De Wolfe (ed.), *Touched with Fire: Civil War Letters and Diary of Oliver Wendell Holmes* (1946).

Jerrold, Blanchard, *The Life of Napoleon III* (1874).
John, Evan (Capt. E. J. Simpson), *Atlantic Impact, 1861* (1952).
Johnson, Albert E. H., "Reminiscences of the Hon. Edwin M. Stanton, Secretary of War," *Records of the Columbia Historical Society*, Vol. 13 (1910).

Lamon, Ward Hill, *Recollections of Abraham Lincoln* (1911).
Leech, Margaret, *Reveille in Washington, 1860-65* (1941).
Loliée, Frédéric, *Les Femmes du Second Empire* (1906).
——, *The Life of an Empress* (1908).
Long, E. B. See Eisenschiml, Otto.
Lorant, Stefan, *The Life of Abraham Lincoln* (1954).
Ludwig, Emil, *Abraham Lincoln* (1949).

Martin, Sir Theodore, *Life of the Prince Consort* (1875-1880).
Massachusetts Historical Society, *Proceedings* (1907-8).
McElroy, Robert, *Jefferson Davis, The Unreal and the Real* (1937).
Mearns, David C., *The Lincoln Papers* (1948).
Metternich, Princess Pauline, *Éclairs du Passé* (1922).
Monaghan, Jay, "Did Abraham Lincoln Receive the Illinois German Vote?" *Jour. Ill. S. H. S.* (1942).

National Archives, Washington.
Nevins, Allan, *Ordeal of the Union* (1947-1950).
——, *The Statesmanship of the Civil War* (1953).
——, *The Improvised War* (1960).
Newman, Ralph. See Eisenschiml, Otto.
Nicolay, Helen, *Personal Traits of Abraham Lincoln* (1912).
Nicolay, John G., and John Hay, *Abraham Lincoln* (1890).

Owsley, Frank Lawrence, *King Cotton Diplomacy* (1931).

Paléologue, George Maurice, *Cavour* (1927).

——, *The Tragic Empress* (1928).

Paris, Louis Philippe Albert d'Orléans, Comte de, *History of the Civil War in America* (1875-88).

Pierce, Edward L., *Memoirs and Letters of Charles Sumner* (1877-93).

Pollard, Edward A., *A Life of Jefferson Davis; With a Secret History of the Southern Confederacy* (1869).

Pratt, Fletcher, *Stanton: Lincoln's Secretary of War* (1953).

Randall, J. G., *Lincoln, the President* (1945-55): Vols. I and II, *Springfield to Gettysburg;* Vol. III, *Midstream;* (with Richard N. Current) Vol. IV, *Last Full Measure.*

Rhodes, James Ford, *History of the Civil War* (1917).

Rippy, J. Fred, *The United States and Mexico* (1931).

Ropes, John Codman, *The Story of the Civil War* (1894-98).

Ruiz, Ramón Eduardo, *The Diaries of William Marshall Anderson* (1959).

Russell, William Howard, "My Diary, North and South" (1863), "Recollections of the Civil War," *North American Review,* Vol. CLXVI (1898).

Salomon, Henry, *L'Ambassade de Richard Metternich á Paris* (1931).

Sandburg, Carl, *Abraham Lincoln: The Prairie Years* (1926).

——, *Abraham Lincoln: The War Years* (1939).

Sanders, Lloyd C., *The Life of Viscount Palmerston* (1895).

Schlesinger, Arthur M., Jr., "The Causes of the Civil War," *Partisan Review* (1949).

Schurz, Carl, *Reminiscences* (1909).

Sears, Louis M., *John Slidell, A Confederate Diplomat at the Court of Napoleon III* (1925).

——, *A History of American Foreign Relations* (1936).

Seward, Frederick W., *Reminiscences of a War-Time Statesman and Diplomat* (1916).

——, *Seward at Washington* (1891).

Stephens, Alexander H., *Recollections: His Diary* (1910).

Stephenson, Nathaniel Wright, *The Autobiography of Abraham Lincoln* (1926).

Thomas, Benjamin P., *Abraham Lincoln: A Biography* (1952).

Union and Confederate Navies, Official Records (1861-65).

Viel-Castel, Horace, Comte de, *Mémoires sur la Règne de Napoléon III* (1883).

Walpole, Spencer, *The Life of Lord John Russell* (1889).
Welles, Gideon, *Diary* (1911).
——, *Lincoln and Seward* (1874).
Wheare, K. C., *Abraham Lincoln and the United States* (1949).
White Collection of Pamphlets, Cornell University Library.
Williams, T. Harry, *Lincoln and His Generals* (1952).

Zornow, William Frank, *Lincoln and the Party Divided* (1954).

Index

Labastida, Archbishop, 24
Laboulaye, Edouard, 82
Lee, Robert E., 37, 127; suggests enlistment of Negroes, 87
Leopold I, King, 109, 151; advises Maximilian, 68-71, 73-74, 78, 110
Lincoln, Abraham, 80, 98, 99, 142, 166; assassination of, 128, 129-33; attitude toward rebels of, 127-28, 133-34; attitude toward slavery of, 43; Burlingame incident and, 32-34; compared to Jefferson Davis, 13-16; elected president, 16; gibed at by Eugénie, 62; hailed in Europe, 82; Hardy's opinion of, 101; Maximilian and, 110-11; and Mexican adventure, 44-50, 134; "one war at a time" policy of, 32, 111; pacifism of, 30; in peace negotiations, 116-17, 121; as personification of republicanism, xv; re-elected, 120; Schurz' opinion of, 31; supports European revolutionaries, 26-29, 33; and *Trent* affair, 41
Lindsay, William S., 85-86
London Conference, 45-46
Loosey, Chevalier Carl F. von, 122-25, 144-45
Louis I, King, 7
Ludwig Victor, Archduke, 105-07

McClellan, George B., 30, 38, 120
Mann, A. Dudley, 17
Mason, James M., 77; *see also Trent* incident
Mathilde, Princess, 52-53
Maximilian, Emperor, xv-xvi, 47, 90, 122, 141; attempts *rapprochement* with Johnson, 138-39, 142-45, 146-48; background of, 65-67; counseled

by Leopold I, 68-71, 73-74, 78, 110; diplomacy of, 105-11; dubbed "Archdupe," 118-19; installed as emperor, 104; last days of, 149-54; and proposed Confederate colonization, 134-36; proposed for emperor, 71-73, 88; raises army, 111-12; renounces Austrian throne, 114-15; supports Confederacy, 79, 110; weakness of, 119-20
Maury, Matthew Fontaine, 135
Mejia, General, 112, 153, 154
Mensdorff-Pouilly, Count, 136
Mercier, Ambassador, 108
Metternich, Prince Richard, 61-62, 86, 126, 160; advises alliance with Napoleon, 64-65; on *Trent* affair, 40-41
Metternich-Winneburg, Prince Clemens Wenzel, 8-9, 65; policy of, 5
Mexico: Confederacy and, 80-82, 88-92, 110, 134-36; "debt collection" expedition to, 44-50; financial interests in, 57-58, 108; French troops in, 85, 87, 103-04, 138; Hardy's discussion of, 91-92; plan to unite Union and Confederacy in war for, 117; slavery in, 89; *see also* Maximilian
Miramón, Gen. Miguel, 23, 24, 57-58, 153, 154
Mormons, 99-100
Morny, Duke of, 51, 79, 108-09; death of, 151; speculations of, 57-58
Motley, John Lothrop, 25, 34-35
Muelinen, Count Rudolf von, 45, 59-61

Napoleon III, Emperor, 12, 29, 40, 118, 148; American experience of, 52; attempts Civil War mediation, 83-86, 88; be-